Pin to Profit : Mastering the Art of Monetizing Pinterest

Introduction

In the bustling world of social media platforms, Pinterest often stands out, not just for its unique visual-driven interface but also for its untapped potential for businesses and individual entrepreneurs. What started as a simple digital pinboard for hobbies and inspirations has transformed into a powerful tool for brand marketing, audience engagement, and, most importantly, monetization.

Many underestimate Pinterest, relegating it to a space for DIY enthusiasts or those seeking wedding inspirations. However, beneath its colorful surface lies a potent platform with over 400 million active users, most of whom are ready to be engaged, influenced, and directed towards products, services, and content. With its unique demographic and user intent, Pinterest users aren't just looking for inspiration; they're often in the mindset to act on their interests, making it a goldmine for savvy marketers and content creators.

As we delve deeper into this guide, we'll uncover the multifaceted aspects of Pinterest, from setting up an impactful profile to creating pins that not only catch the eye but also drive action. Monetizing Pinterest is more than just pinning random images; it requires strategy, understanding of the platform's algorithm, and a genuine connection with the audience.

This journey won't merely be about theory. Along the way, you'll encounter actionable steps, real-world examples, tools, and strategies designed to transform your Pinterest presence from a casual pastime to a genuine profit-making venture. Whether you're an individual looking to drive traffic to your blog, an entrepreneur hoping to boost product sales, or a

1

brand seeking increased visibility, this guide holds the keys to unlocking Pinterest's potential.

As we start this exciting exploration, let's first delve into the core basics of Pinterest. By grasping the foundational elements, we'll be better equipped to navigate the intricate maze of monetization strategies that lie ahead.

Understanding Pinterest at its core is akin to learning the rules of a game. By mastering the foundational principles, we set the stage for advanced tactics and strategies. It's more than just about knowing where to click or how to create a board; it's about comprehending the mindset of Pinterest users, recognizing the trends that drive engagement, and leveraging these insights for monetization.

Furthermore, as a platform that's constantly evolving, keeping up with Pinterest's shifts and changes is crucial. But fret not; this guide aims to be your compass in this ever-changing landscape, providing timely advice and actionable steps regardless of the platform's updates.

However, before we get into the nitty-gritty of monetization, there's immense value in appreciating the journey. Monetizing any platform, Pinterest included, is not an overnight venture. It requires patience, consistency, and a commitment to delivering value to your audience. Every pin you post, every board you create, and every interaction you have on the platform should be underscored by a genuine desire to serve and engage your audience. When this mindset is in place, the strategies we'll explore will not only make sense but will also yield fruitful results.

So, as we embark on this comprehensive journey from 'Pin to Profit', let's first ground ourselves in the essential world of Pinterest Basics, ensuring that our foundation is robust, enabling us to build a successful monetization strategy atop it.

Chapter 1: Pinterest Basics

In the realm of social media, where platforms like Facebook, Instagram, and Twitter often dominate the conversation, Pinterest carves out a unique niche for itself. Unlike other platforms where the primary focus might be on status updates, sharing life moments, or following news, Pinterest is inherently about discovery, inspiration, and action.

Understanding the Pinterest Landscape

To truly harness the potential of Pinterest for monetization, we must first familiarize ourselves with its foundational elements.

- Pins: At the heart of Pinterest are Pins. Think of a Pin as a visual bookmark, a way to save something you find on the web or directly on Pinterest. Each Pin links back to its source, be it a blog, a product page, or any other website, making it a powerful tool for driving traffic.

- Boards: Pins are organized into Boards. A Board is a collection of Pins, usually centered around a specific topic or theme. For example, if you're in the home décor niche, you might have separate Boards for 'Living Room Inspirations', 'Kitchen Designs', and 'Bedroom Decor Ideas'.

- Feed: Just like other social media platforms, when you log into Pinterest, you're greeted by a feed. This feed is a mix of Pins from users you follow, suggested Pins based on your activity, and promoted Pins (ads).

- Profiles: Each user on Pinterest has a profile, where their Boards and Pins are displayed. This is also where you can see who they follow and who follows them. For businesses and content creators, an optimized profile is essential for attracting followers and driving engagement.

- Search and Discovery: Pinterest is as much a search engine as it is a social platform. People come to Pinterest to search for ideas, making keyword optimization crucial for visibility.

Setting Up an Optimal Profile

Your Pinterest profile serves as the first impression for many users. Whether they stumble upon one of your Pins in their feed or they directly search for your profile, how you present yourself can make a significant difference in gaining a follower or driving a click to your website.

1. Profile Picture: Use a high-quality image, ideally a logo for brands or a professional headshot for individual creators. Ensure the image is clear even on mobile devices.

2.   Username and Display Name: Your username will be part of your Pinterest URL, so choose something memorable and related to your brand or niche. The display name offers more flexibility; you can use it to highlight your niche or specialty. For instance, "Jane Doe | Home Décor Enthusiast" gives a clear indication of the profile's focus.

3.   Bio: Your bio should be concise, yet informative. Use this space to tell visitors what you're about and what value you offer. Incorporate keywords related to your niche, as Pinterest bios are searchable.

4.   Website Link: If you have a blog, online store, or any website, link it. This not only drives traffic but also adds credibility to your profile. Additionally, consider verifying your website with Pinterest. Verified profiles have a checkmark next to their domain, signaling authenticity to users.

5.   Board Organization: Your Boards should reflect your brand or content areas. Consider the aesthetics and organization. Place your most important or popular Boards at the top. Use clear, descriptive names for Boards, and optimize the descriptions with relevant keywords.

The Importance of Pinterest SEO

Search Engine Optimization (SEO) isn't just for Google. Pinterest, with its search and discovery mechanism, also relies heavily on keywords to show relevant content to its users. This makes understanding and implementing Pinterest SEO techniques fundamental for anyone looking to drive traffic and engagement.

1.   Keyword Research: Start by typing potential keywords into the Pinterest search bar and note the auto-suggestions. These suggestions provide insight into popular search queries. You can also explore the 'Trending' section to see what's currently popular on Pinterest.

2.   Optimizing Pins: Use keywords in your Pin titles and descriptions. This increases the chances of your Pins appearing in relevant search results. However, ensure the descriptions sound natural and provide value to the reader.

3.   Board Descriptions: Just as with Pins, optimizing Board names and descriptions with relevant keywords can increase their visibility in search results.

4.   Profile Optimization: We touched on this earlier, but it's worth reiterating: use keywords in your profile name and bio. It can make your profile more discoverable to users interested in your niche.

5.   Image Optimization: Pinterest is a visual platform, so the images you pin should be high-quality, vertical (a 2:3 aspect ratio is often recommended), and relevant to the content. While the algorithm doesn't "read" the image, a relevant and eye-catching image can increase user engagement, signaling to Pinterest that your content is valuable.

Understanding these basic elements and implementing foundational strategies are the stepping stones to mastering Pinterest. As we progress, you'll see how these basics integrate into more advanced techniques, from affiliate marketing to driving significant web traffic.

However, even with a strong grasp of the basics, achieving tangible results requires more than just knowledge. It demands strategic action. In the next section, we'll dive into building an engaging Pinterest profile, a cornerstone for any successful monetization endeavor.

The Art of Crafting Perfect Pins

The core of Pinterest is its Pins. Creating the perfect Pin isn't just about choosing a pretty picture; it's a blend of visuals, compelling descriptions, and strategic placements. Let's delve deeper into the anatomy of a perfect Pin.

1.   Visual Aesthetics: Considering Pinterest is a visual platform, the image you choose is paramount. Go for high-resolution images that resonate with your target audience. Vibrant colors, particularly reds and oranges, tend to perform well. Ensure your image speaks to the content it represents. For product pins, clear product shots against a contrasting background or lifestyle images showing the product in use can be effective.

2.   Text Overlays: Sometimes, an image alone isn't enough to convey your message. Text overlays can provide context. If you're sharing a blog post titled "10 Home Décor Hacks," an overlay with that title can make the Pin's purpose

clear. Use legible fonts and maintain a balance between image and text.

3.   Pin Descriptions: Your Pin's description should be engaging and informative. It's your opportunity to entice the viewer to click through. Integrate keywords naturally, provide context, and whenever applicable, include a call-to-action like "Click to discover more" or "Find out how."

4.   Rich Pins: These are Pins that include extra information. For instance, an article Rich Pin might show the headline, author, and a story description. For products, it could show the price and availability. Rich Pins stand out and provide additional context, which can boost engagement.

5.   Pin Dimensions: Vertical pins work best, as they take up more real estate on users' feeds. A 2:3 aspect ratio, like 600x900 pixels, is generally recommended.

Engaging with the Pinterest Community

Monetization is not just about broadcasting your content; it's about genuine engagement. Being an active part of the Pinterest community can have numerous benefits.

1.   Commenting: Engage with Pins in your niche by leaving thoughtful comments. It can drive users to check out your profile.

2.   Collaborative Boards: These are boards where multiple users can pin. Joining or creating collaborative boards in your niche can increase your reach.

3.   Repins and Curated Content: Don't just pin your content. By repinning relevant content from others, you show your audience that you're active and invested in providing value. It also fosters a sense of community, and those you repin might return the favor.

4.   Engaging Responsively: If someone comments on your pin or sends you a message, make an effort to respond. Building relationships can lead to loyal followers and increased engagement.

Tailoring Content for a Global Audience

Pinterest has a vast international audience. If you're aiming to monetize on a larger scale, considering global trends and preferences can be beneficial.

1.   Cultural Sensitivity: Understand that what's popular or acceptable in one culture might not be in another.

2.   Seasonal Considerations: While it's summer in the U.S., it's winter in Australia. If you're targeting a global audience, be mindful of seasonal discrepancies.

3.   Language and Terminology: If a significant portion of your audience comes from a non-English speaking country, consider creating Pins in that language. Even for English speakers, be mindful of terminology differences (e.g., "trousers" in the UK vs. "pants" in the US).

Analyzing Your Performance with Pinterest Analytics

You can't improve what you don't measure. Pinterest offers robust analytics for business accounts, providing insights into how your Pins and boards are performing.

1.   Overview: Understand your profile's overall performance. How many views are your Pins getting? How many clicks?

2.   Audience Insights: Discover more about your audience. What are their interests? Where are they located?

3.   Top Pins: Identify which Pins are driving the most engagement. This can help you understand what's resonating with your audience and tailor your strategy accordingly.

By mastering these foundational aspects of Pinterest, you're setting the stage for success. While it's tempting to dive straight into monetization strategies, grounding yourself in the basics ensures that when you do start implementing advanced techniques, they're built on a solid foundation.

In the next chapter, we'll explore the various avenues for monetizing Pinterest, from affiliate marketing to sponsored content. Each strategy comes with its nuances, and by leveraging the insights and skills you've acquired from this chapter, you'll be well-equipped to navigate the exciting journey from 'Pin to Profit'.

Chapter 2: Monetizing Pinterest - From Inspiration to Income

Having a strong grasp of Pinterest's basics is crucial, but knowing how to strategically monetize the platform is where the real magic happens. In this chapter, we'll explore the various avenues available to transform your Pinterest presence from a hobby or brand showcase into a potential income stream.

1. Affiliate Marketing on Pinterest

Affiliate marketing is the practice of promoting products or services for others and earning a commission for every sale or action made through your referral. Pinterest can be an effective platform for this.

- Choosing the Right Program: Opt for affiliate programs that align with your niche. If you're into fashion, programs from clothing brands or fashion retailers might be suitable.
- Creating Authentic Pins: Your Pins should feel genuine. Instead of just pinning product images, create Pins that showcase the product in real-life contexts. For fashion, it could be a person wearing the item. For tech, it might be the gadget being used.
- Disclose Affiliate Links: Transparency is key. Ensure you disclose any affiliate links to your followers, either by mentioning it in the Pin description or using hashtags like #affiliate or #ad.
- Track Performance: Use tracking links to gauge which Pins are driving sales. This will help you refine your strategy over time.

2. Sponsored Pins and Partnerships

Brands are always on the lookout for popular Pinterest users to collaborate with to reach a wider audience.

- Engage with Brands: If you have a substantial following, brands might approach you. But there's no harm in reaching out to brands that align with your content.

- Craft Genuine Content: Even if you're getting paid, ensure the Pins you create resonate with your audience and feel authentic.
- Full Disclosure: As with affiliate marketing, always disclose sponsored content to maintain trust with your followers.

3. Driving Traffic to Monetized Content

Pinterest can be a significant traffic driver to your blog or website, where you might have other monetization methods in place, such as ads or e-commerce.

- Optimized Pin Descriptions: Craft descriptions that entice users to click through. If you're sharing a blog post, provide a teaser or highlight the value they'll get by visiting.
- Rich Pins for Articles: Use article Rich Pins to provide more context about your blog post directly on Pinterest.
- Consistent Branding: Ensure there's a visual consistency between your Pins and your website to provide a seamless user experience.

4. Selling Products Directly

If you have an online store, Pinterest can be a direct sales channel.

- Product Pins: These Pins display the price and a direct link to the product page on your website, streamlining the shopping process.
- Seasonal and Trend-Based Pins: If it's the holiday season, Pin gift ideas from your store. If a particular product is trending, create dedicated Pins for it.
- Engaging Imagery: Use images that show the product in use, offering potential buyers a glimpse into how it fits into their lives.

5. Offering Pinterest Management Services

If you've mastered Pinterest, consider offering your expertise as a service.

- Package Your Services: Offer packages like Pinterest profile optimization, monthly pinning, or complete Pinterest management.

- Showcase Your Success: Use your Pinterest profile as a portfolio, highlighting your growth and engagement metrics to attract potential clients.

6. Teaching and Consulting

Share your Pinterest expertise through courses, workshops, or one-on-one consultations.

- Online Courses: Platforms like Teachable or Udemy allow you to host and sell courses. Create comprehensive courses on Pinterest strategies, from basics to advanced monetization.
- Workshops: Consider live workshops, either in-person or online. These can be deep dives into specific areas of Pinterest.
- Consultations: Offer personalized advice and strategies through one-on-one consulting sessions.

7. Promoted Pins: Paid Advertising on Pinterest

While organic reach is impressive on Pinterest, using Promoted Pins can help you target a specific audience and accelerate your monetization efforts.

- Setting Goals: Before promoting a Pin, define your objective. Is it brand awareness, website traffic, or conversions you're aiming for?
- Targeting: Pinterest's ad platform offers robust targeting options. Define your audience based on demographics, interests, or even certain keywords.
- Budgeting and Bidding: Determine your daily or lifetime budget for the ad campaign. Remember to monitor and adjust bids based on performance.
- Analytics: Use Pinterest's ad analytics to evaluate the performance of your Promoted Pins. Track metrics like impressions, clicks, saves, and, most importantly, the return on ad spend (ROAS).

8. Hosting Pinterest Webinars and Live Sessions

The appeal of live sessions has grown across various platforms. Use this trend to your advantage.

- Topics of Interest: Host webinars on 'How to grow your Pinterest following' or 'Mastering Pinterest SEO'. Ensure the topic offers value and resonates with your audience.

- Promotion: Use your other social media platforms, email list, and, of course, Pinterest itself, to promote upcoming webinars.
- Monetization: Offer the webinar for free to build a community but consider having a premium segment or exclusive downloadable resources for a fee.

9. Licensing Your Popular Pins

If you're a content creator and some of your Pins gain significant traction, brands might be interested in licensing them for their marketing campaigns.

- Watermark Your Original Content: To ensure your content isn't misused, always watermark original images or infographics.
- Engage with Interested Parties: If a brand expresses interest, negotiate terms that are mutually beneficial.
- Stay Updated with Licensing Laws: Understand the basics of image licensing to ensure you're not shortchanging yourself.

10. Cross-Promotion with Other Platforms

Your Pinterest audience can be directed to other monetized platforms or vice versa.

- YouTube and Pinterest: If you have monetized YouTube content, create Pins that lead to your videos. Alternatively, promote your Pinterest boards in your video descriptions or pinned comments.
- Newsletter Sign-ups: Direct Pinterest traffic to sign up for your email newsletter, which can have its monetization strategies, like affiliate links or sponsored content.
- Instagram and Pinterest: Cross-promote between these visual platforms. A Pin could lead to an Instagram post or IGTV video, while your Instagram Stories could promote your Pinterest boards.

Wrapping Up the Chapter

While Pinterest might appear, at first glance, to be a simple platform for inspiration, its potential as a monetization powerhouse is undeniable. From direct sales to affiliate marketing, paid advertising to content licensing, the possibilities are diverse. The key lies in understanding the platform's nuances, being genuine in your engagement, and continuously adapting to its evolving dynamics.

By now, you should have a holistic view of the monetization avenues available on Pinterest. As we venture into the next chapters, we'll dive deeper into each strategy, discussing tools, best practices, pitfalls to avoid, and real-life success stories that will inspire and guide your Pinterest journey.

Remember, the Pinterest landscape is vast and ever-evolving. Stay curious, stay engaged, and keep pinning with purpose.

Chapter 3: Affiliate Marketing Deep Dive: Turning Pins into Profit

Affiliate marketing remains one of the most popular and viable monetization strategies on Pinterest. This chapter aims to take a closer look, guiding you through the intricate maze of affiliate marketing on Pinterest, ensuring you not only understand the nuances but also master the art.

1. Understanding Affiliate Marketing

• Basics Unveiled: At its core, affiliate marketing is about promoting products or services for a commission. Every sale or action made through your referral earns you a piece of the profit.

• Commission Structures: Familiarize yourself with the different structures. Some programs offer a flat rate per sale, while others might offer a percentage of the sale amount.

2. Choosing the Right Affiliate Programs

• Niche Relevance: The affiliate program you choose should align with your Pinterest content. Promoting irrelevant products can feel forced and reduce trust among followers.

• Reputation and Reviews: Research potential programs. Look for reviews from other affiliates and check the program's reputation.

• Payout Details: Understand the payout threshold, payment3. Creating High-Converting Pins

- Authentic Imagery: Use images that resonate with your audience. If possible, use the product and take original photos.
- Compelling Descriptions: Craft descriptions that highlight the product's benefits and reasons to purchase.
- Clear Call-to-Action (CTA): Encourage users to click through with a clear CTA like "Find out more" or "Shop now."

4. Disclosures and Ethical Considerations
- Transparency is Key: Always disclose affiliate links. Not only is it ethical, but it's also often required by law.
- Building Trust: Being upfront about affiliate links can enhance trust with your audience. They appreciate honesty and transparency.

5. Maximizing Affiliate Earnings
- Regularly Update Pins: Product availability, prices, or offers might change. Regularly review and update your Pins to ensure accuracy.
- Seasonal and Event-Based Promotions: Leverage holidays or events (like Black Friday) to promote relevant products.
- Engage with Comments: If users comment on your Pins asking for more information or reviews, engage with them. This can increase the likelihood of conversions.

6. Combining Affiliate Marketing with Other Strategies
- Blog Integration: Drive Pinterest traffic to blog posts that include affiliate links. This provides an additional touchpoint before the purchase.
- Email Marketing: Consider promoting affiliate products in your email newsletters, leveraging the traffic you've driven from Pinterest.

7. Case Study: A Pinterest Affiliate Marketing Success
- Background: Dive into a real-life example of a Pinterest user who successfully leveraged affiliate marketing.
- Strategies Adopted: Understand the specific tactics they employed, from Pin design to engagement strategies.
- Results: Analyze the outcomes, both in terms of engagement and revenue generated.

8. Potential Pitfalls and How to Avoid Them

- Over-Promotion: Bombarding your followers with affiliate Pins can be off-putting. Strive for a balance between promotional and non-promotional content.
- Not Tracking Performance: Use tracking links and regularly review analytics to understand what's working and what's not.
- Ignoring Feedback: If followers express concerns or dissatisfaction with a product you're promoting, listen and consider adjusting your strategy.

9. Tools and Resources for Affiliate Marketers on Pinterest

- Affiliate Dashboards: Many affiliate programs offer dashboards that provide real-time insights into click-through rates, conversions, and earnings. Familiarize yourself with these to monitor your progress.
- Pinterest Analytics: Keep an eye on the performance of your Pins. Which ones are getting the most clicks, saves, and conversions? This data can guide your future strategy.
- Link Shorteners with Tracking: Tools like Bitly can help you create cleaner looking links while also offering tracking capabilities.

10. Engaging and Growing Your Audience

- Pin Consistently: The more active you are on Pinterest, the more visibility you'll gain. Set aside time each week to curate and pin content.
- Join Group Boards: Collaborative boards with a significant following can amplify your reach. Share your affiliate Pins here, but ensure they're relevant to the board's theme.
- Engage with Other Pinners: Comment on, save, and engage with Pins from others in your niche. This can drive reciprocal engagement and increase your visibility.

11. Diversifying Affiliate Streams

- Multiple Programs: Don't put all your eggs in one basket. Join multiple affiliate programs to diversify your income streams.
- Different Product Categories: If you primarily promote fashion items, consider branching out into related niches, like beauty or accessories.

- International Opportunities: Some products might have global appeal. Explore affiliate programs that cater to international audiences or offer worldwide shipping.

12. Staying Updated with Trends and Best Practices

- Affiliate Marketing News and Updates: Subscribe to industry newsletters or blogs. This keeps you informed about any changes in regulations or best practices.
- Pinterest Updates: Stay abreast of any changes Pinterest makes to its platform, algorithms, or policies. Such changes can impact your affiliate marketing efforts.
- Continuous Learning: Consider enrolling in advanced affiliate marketing courses or workshops to further hone your skills.

13. Challenges in Affiliate Marketing on Pinterest and Overcoming Them

- Saturation: As more users jump on the affiliate marketing bandwagon, there's a risk of saturating your niche. Overcome this by focusing on unique, high-quality content and genuine engagement.
- Changing Algorithms: Like all platforms, Pinterest's algorithms change. This can impact visibility. Counteract this by staying updated and being willing to adapt.
- Trust Issues: With the rise of affiliate marketing, some users have grown wary. Prioritize transparency and genuine recommendations to maintain trust.

Concluding Thoughts for Chapter 3

Venturing into affiliate marketing on Pinterest can seem daunting, but with the right strategies, tools, and mindset, it offers a wealth of opportunities. The key is to prioritize authenticity, continuously learn, and be adaptable. Your followers on Pinterest are seeking inspiration and recommendations; by offering genuine value and transparently sharing products and services that resonate, you can cultivate a loyal audience and a sustainable income stream.

In the chapters ahead, we'll dive deeper into other avenues of monetization on Pinterest, like sponsored content, e-commerce integration, and more. Each strategy offers its unique set of advantages, challenges, and nuances. Together, they paint a comprehensive picture of the potential Pinterest holds for creators and brands alike.

Chapter 4: E-Commerce Integration: Transforming Pins into Direct Sales

Pinterest's visual nature makes it an ideal platform for e-commerce brands and businesses. This chapter delves into the world of integrating e-commerce with Pinterest, allowing for direct sales from pins and transforming followers into customers.

1. The Power of Pinterest for E-Commerce
- Shopping Inspiration: Pinterest users often visit the platform in search of shopping inspiration, making it a prime audience for e-commerce businesses.
- Visual Showcase: Presenting products in a visually appealing manner can significantly boost their attractiveness to potential buyers.

2. Setting Up a Pinterest Business Account
- Business vs. Personal: Understand the advantages a business account offers, such as rich pins, analytics, and advertising options.
- Profile Optimization: Make sure your profile clearly communicates your brand identity, complete with a logo, business description, and a link to your online store.

3. Rich Pins and Product Pins
- Introduction to Rich Pins: These are pins that include extra information right on the pin itself. For e-commerce, product pins are particularly valuable.
- Advantages of Product Pins: Product pins include real-time pricing, availability, and where to buy. This makes the shopping experience seamless for Pinterest users.

4. Crafting Pins That Sell
- High-Quality Imagery: Ensure product photos are clear, high-resolution, and showcase the product's features.

- Engaging Descriptions: Craft descriptions that highlight the product benefits and entice users to click through.
- Promotions and Offers: Highlight any ongoing promotions, discounts, or exclusive offers to incentivize pinners to make a purchase.

5. Driving Traffic to Your Online Store
- Optimize for Click-Throughs: Make sure your pins are designed to drive traffic to your product pages.
- Seamless User Experience: Ensure that the transition from Pinterest to your online store is smooth. Mobile optimization is crucial, given Pinterest's high mobile user base.

6. Pinterest Shopping Ads
- Benefits of Shopping Ads: These ads automatically create promoted pins from your product listing, saving you time.
- Targeting and Retargeting: Utilize Pinterest's targeting options to reach potential customers. Consider retargeting users who've visited your site but didn't make a purchase.

7. Using Pinterest Analytics for E-Commerce Insights
- Track Performance: Monitor which pins are driving the most traffic and sales to adjust your strategy accordingly.
- Audience Insights: Understand your audience demographics, preferences, and behavior to tailor your e-commerce approach on Pinterest.

8. Collaborations and Partnerships
- Partner with Influencers: Collaborate with Pinterest influencers to showcase your products to a broader audience.
- Join Group Boards: Participate in or create group boards relevant to your product niche, expanding your reach.

9. Case Study: E-Commerce Success on Pinterest
- Background: A real-life example of a brand that effectively leveraged Pinterest for e-commerce growth.
- Strategies Used: Dive into the specific tactics and methodologies they employed.
- Outcome: Analyze the results in terms of traffic, sales, and brand awareness.

10. Challenges and Overcoming Them
- Competitive Landscape: With many brands vying for attention, stand out by emphasizing uniqueness.
- Changing User Behavior: Stay attuned to shifts in how users engage with e-commerce on Pinterest. Adapt your strategy as needed.
- Technical Glitches: Ensure your website is prepared for potential traffic surges from Pinterest to prevent site crashes.

11. Customer Engagement and Building Loyalty
- Engaging Descriptions: Go beyond product features. Tell a story that resonates with your audience's aspirations and lifestyles.
- User-Generated Content: Encourage satisfied customers to share their product photos. Repin and celebrate this content to build a community feeling.
- Prompt Response: Engage with comments, questions, and feedback on your Pins. A quick and helpful response can improve brand perception and loyalty.

12. Seasonal and Event-based Promotions on Pinterest
- Holiday Themes: Adjust your Pin aesthetics and promotions according to the season or upcoming holidays. For instance, during the holiday season, curate a board with gift ideas.
- Flash Sales and Exclusive Offers: Create time-sensitive promotions exclusive for your Pinterest followers. This not only boosts sales but also incentivizes users to follow and engage with your brand on Pinterest.

13. Integrating with E-Commerce Platforms
- Shopify and Pinterest: If you're using Shopify, explore the Pinterest integration. This can streamline the process of listing products on Pinterest.
- Other Integrations: Platforms like WooCommerce, BigCommerce, and Magento often have plugins or tools that make integration with Pinterest easier.

14. Mobile Optimization
- The Significance: A considerable chunk of Pinterest users access the platform via mobile. Ensure that the shopping experience is optimized for mobile devices.

- Quick Load Times: Ensure your product pages load quickly to reduce bounce rates.
- Mobile-Friendly Checkout: Simplify the checkout process on mobile. Consider integrating popular mobile payment methods.

15. Measuring ROI and Performance Metrics
- Key Metrics: Track metrics like click-through rates, conversion rates, average order value, and customer lifetime value specifically from Pinterest traffic.
- ROI Calculation: Deduct your Pinterest-related expenses (like ads, promotions, or influencer partnerships) from the revenue generated via Pinterest. This gives you a clear picture of your return on investment.
- Adapt and Optimize: Regularly review performance data and adjust your strategies for continuous improvement.

16. Future Outlook: What's Next for Pinterest and E-Commerce?
- Emerging Trends: Stay updated with the evolving shopping trends on Pinterest. For instance, the rise of video Pins can be a game-changer for product showcases.
- Augmented Reality (AR) and Pinterest: Explore the potential of AR in the context of Pinterest shopping. AR can enhance the shopping experience by allowing users to "try on" products virtually.
- Building an Omnichannel Experience: Consider integrating Pinterest with other social media shopping experiences for a seamless omnichannel approach.

Concluding Thoughts for Chapter 4

The marriage between Pinterest and e-commerce is a match made in digital heaven. Brands that can seamlessly blend the visual appeal of their products with the aspirational essence of Pinterest stand to gain significantly. It's about creating not just a shopping platform but an experience that resonates deeply with Pinterest's user base.

As we transition into the subsequent chapters, we'll delve into further dimensions of Pinterest monetization. From harnessing the potential of videos to understanding the dynamics of sponsored partnerships, our journey into the world of Pinterest profitability continues.

Chapter 5: Harnessing the Power of Video: The Rise of Pinterest Video Pins

With the continuous evolution of Pinterest, video content has emerged as a compelling medium for creators and businesses alike. This chapter will guide you through leveraging video pins for monetization, understanding its potential, and ensuring maximum reach and engagement.

1. Understanding the Significance of Video on Pinterest
- User Engagement: Why video content captivates Pinterest users more than static images.
- Telling a Story: The power of video in conveying a brand's story, product usage, or a tutorial in a concise, engaging manner.

2. Getting Started with Video Pins
- Setting Up: Basics of creating a video pin – from uploading to crafting an effective description.
- Technical Specifications: Understanding video formats, resolution, aspect ratios, and length suitable for Pinterest.

3. Crafting Compelling Video Content
- Quality Over Quantity: Importance of high-definition, clear videos that resonate with your target audience.
- Storyboarding: Planning your video content to ensure it conveys the desired message effectively.
- Incorporate Branding: Subtly adding your brand's logo or colors to maintain brand consistency.

4. Video Descriptions That Drive Action
- Clear CTAs: Encouraging users to take action, whether it's visiting a website, purchasing a product, or signing up for a newsletter.
- SEO Optimized: Incorporate keywords relevant to your video content to ensure discoverability.
- Engage with Comments: Foster community and engagement by responding to user comments and feedback on your video pins.

5. Tutorials and How-To Videos

- **DIY Popularity:** Leveraging the trend of DIY and how-to videos on Pinterest.
- **Product Demonstrations:** Showcasing your product in action, highlighting its features and benefits.
- **Interactive Workshops:** Engaging users with longer, workshop-style video content that provides in-depth information or skills.

6. Promoted Video Pins

- **Paid Reach:** Enhancing your video's reach and visibility through Pinterest's promoted video options.
- **Targeting:** Ensuring your video content reaches the right audience through precise targeting options.
- **Analyzing Performance:** Utilizing Pinterest analytics to understand your promoted video's performance and ROI.

7. Integrating E-Commerce with Video Pins

- **Shoppable Videos:** Creating video content that directly links to products, making the shopping experience seamless.
- **Testimonials and Reviews:** Featuring real-life users sharing their positive experiences with your product or service.

8. Challenges of Video Content on Pinterest

- **Standing Out:** Crafting unique content in an increasingly saturated video landscape.
- **Staying Updated:** Keeping abreast of changing trends, user preferences, and platform updates.
- **Technical Issues:** Overcoming potential technical glitches, such as optimizing video load times for mobile users.

9. Case Study: Success with Pinterest Video Content

- **Background:** Introduction to a brand or creator who has effectively used video content on Pinterest.
- **Strategies Employed:** A deep dive into the tactics, video types, and promotional methods they used.
- **Results Achieved:** Analyzing the outcomes in terms of engagement, reach, conversions, and brand visibility.

10. Future of Video on Pinterest

- **Emerging Trends:** Exploring upcoming video trends on Pinterest, like augmented reality integrations or interactive video features.

- Platform Innovations: Staying updated with any new tools, features, or specifications introduced by Pinterest for video content.
- Cross-platform Synergy: Integrating Pinterest video strategies with other social media platforms for a holistic video marketing approach.

11. Collaborating with Video Influencers on Pinterest
- Finding the Right Fit: Identifying influencers whose style, audience, and values align with your brand.
- Co-Creation: Working with influencers to produce authentic, engaging video content that feels organic rather than promotional.
- Measure and Iterate: Analyzing the results of influencer collaborations to refine future partnerships and strategies.

12. Engaging with Live Video Features
- The Rise of Live Content: Understanding the growing trend of real-time content and its implications on Pinterest.
- Hosting Live Events: Engaging your audience with real-time product launches, Q&A sessions, or behind-the-scenes peeks into your brand.
- Interactivity: Making the most of live sessions by interacting directly with viewers, responding to comments, and driving real-time engagement.

13. Tips for Enhancing Video Engagement
- Captivating Thumbnails: Using visually appealing thumbnails to grab users' attention and increase click-through rates.
- Video Length: Identifying the optimal video duration for your content type and audience's preferences.
- Consistency: Establishing a regular posting schedule to keep your audience engaged and returning for more.

14. Utilizing Pinterest Analytics for Video Insights
- Key Metrics: Delving into video-specific metrics like view duration, engagement rate, and click-through rate.
- Audience Insights: Understanding viewer demographics, behaviors, and preferences to tailor your video content strategy.

• Refinement: Using insights to continuously refine your video content, ensuring it remains relevant and engaging.

15. Integration with Other Video Platforms

• Cross-Promotion: Sharing your Pinterest video content on platforms like YouTube, Instagram, or TikTok to amplify its reach.

• Repurposing Content: Adapting videos created for other platforms to fit Pinterest's format and audience.

• Synergy: Creating a cohesive video strategy across platforms, ensuring brand consistency and a unified narrative.

16. Overcoming Common Video Pitfalls

• Avoiding Over-Promotion: Striking a balance between promotional and value-driven content to avoid alienating your audience.

• Sound and Subtitles: Ensuring your video content is accessible and understandable, even if viewed without sound.

• Staying Updated: Continuously updating skills and equipment to produce high-quality, relevant video content.

17. Community Engagement Through Video

• Challenges and Tutorials: Creating engaging challenges or tutorials that encourage user participation and interaction.

• User-Generated Video Content: Encouraging and curating videos from your audience, building a sense of community and trust.

• Feedback Loops: Using video as a medium to seek feedback on new products or services, making your audience feel valued and involved.

Concluding Thoughts for Chapter 5

Video content on Pinterest offers a plethora of opportunities for brands and creators to deeply connect with their audience. By crafting content that resonates, tells a story, and offers value, you can ensure sustained engagement and effectively drive your monetization goals on the platform.

Our journey into Pinterest's multifaceted world continues. In the subsequent chapters, we'll explore other avenues, from community building to leveraging advanced analytics, ensuring a holistic approach to Pinterest profitability.

Chapter 6: Community Building: Cultivating Loyal Followers and Creating Brand Ambassadors

Building a robust community around your brand on Pinterest isn't just about numbers; it's about nurturing genuine relationships with followers who align with your brand's ethos. This chapter delves into strategies that foster loyalty, engagement, and community-driven growth on Pinterest.

1. The Value of a Dedicated Pinterest Community
  • Beyond Metrics: Understanding that a loyal follower base often leads to better engagement rates, conversion rates, and brand advocacy.
  • Cultivating Brand Loyalty: How a tight-knit community can act as a natural defense against competition.

2. Quality Over Quantity
  • Genuine Followers: The importance of targeting users who genuinely connect with your brand rather than just inflating follower counts.
  • Engagement Metrics: Why higher engagement from a smaller, dedicated community can be more valuable than passive larger audiences.

3. Strategies to Build and Nurture Your Community
  • Consistent Posting: Maintaining a steady flow of quality content that resonates with your audience.
  • Active Engagement: Prioritizing interactions, replying to comments, and acknowledging feedback.
  • User-Generated Content: Celebrating content created by your followers, giving them a sense of ownership and involvement.

4. Creating Value-Driven Content
  • Educational Pins: Offering tutorials, tips, and insights that provide tangible value to your audience.
  • Inspiring Stories: Sharing testimonials, success stories, or motivational narratives that align with your brand's message.
  • Behind-the-Scenes: Giving followers a peek into your brand's processes, team, or work culture.

5. Leveraging Group Boards for Community Interaction
- Collaborative Spaces: Using group boards as a space for followers to share ideas, inspirations, or their own content.
- Moderation and Quality Control: Ensuring the content aligns with the board's theme and your brand's values.

6. Hosting Pinterest Contests and Challenges
- Engagement Boost: Organizing contests that prompt users to create, share, or engage with your brand's content.
- Rewarding Loyalty: Offering exclusive deals, promotions, or giveaways to dedicated followers.

7. Empowering Brand Ambassadors
- Identification: Recognizing and reaching out to loyal followers who consistently engage with and promote your brand.
- Collaboration: Working with these ambassadors on content creation, promotions, or product launches.

8. Tackling Negative Feedback and Criticism
- Constructive Approach: Viewing criticism as an opportunity for improvement and engaging in constructive dialogues.
- Conflict Resolution: Handling negative situations with grace, understanding, and a focus on resolution.

9. Utilizing Analytics for Community Insights
- Demographics and Preferences: Gaining a deeper understanding of who your followers are and what they resonate with.
- Tailored Content: Adjusting your content strategy based on insights to better serve and engage your community.

10. Cross-Promotion with Other Social Platforms
- Holistic Approach: Integrating your Pinterest community-building efforts with other social platforms for a cohesive brand experience.
- Multi-Platform Contests: Organizing activities that span across different platforms, maximizing reach and participation.

11. Hosting Virtual Events or Webinars
- Deep Engagement: Using Pinterest to promote and host virtual events that offer deeper insights, tutorials, or exclusive content.

- Feedback Sessions: Organizing sessions where followers can voice opinions, ask questions, or suggest improvements.

12. Engaging with Trending Topics and Current Events
- Staying Relevant: The significance of aligning your content with current happenings and trending discussions.
- Being Respectful and Authentic: Navigating sensitive topics with care, ensuring your engagement comes across as genuine and not opportunistic.

13. Collaborative Projects with Followers
- Co-creation: Initiating projects where followers can actively contribute, whether it's designs, ideas, or feedback.
- Showcasing Talent: Highlighting exceptional contributions, making followers feel valued and celebrated.

14. Building Trust through Transparency
- Openness in Communication: Sharing challenges, achievements, and future plans, creating a bond of trust with your audience.
- Ethical Practices: Demonstrating commitment to ethical and sustainable practices, which can resonate deeply with a conscientious audience.

15. Organizing Offline Events or Meetups
- Strengthening Bonds: Using Pinterest to promote real-world events, allowing followers to connect with the brand and each other in person.
- Showcasing Products: Offering exclusive previews or sales at these events, enhancing the exclusivity factor.

16. Tailoring Your Communication Style
- Personalized Engagement: Ensuring your brand communication feels personalized and not robotic. This can involve sharing personal anecdotes or using a more conversational tone.
- Feedback Loop: Regularly soliciting feedback on your communication style and making necessary adjustments.

17. Embracing Diversity and Inclusion
- Representation Matters: Highlighting diverse voices, experiences, and perspectives, making every follower feel seen and valued.

- Continuous Learning: Educating oneself and the brand on diverse cultures, backgrounds, and experiences to ensure respectful and inclusive communication.

18. Encouraging Peer-to-Peer Interactions

- Fostering Community Spirit: Encouraging followers to interact with each other, share experiences, and build connections.
- Moderating Discussions: Ensuring that community interactions remain respectful and aligned with the brand's values.

19. Providing Exclusive Content and Perks

- Rewarding Loyalty: Offering early access, exclusive content, or special discounts to dedicated followers.
- VIP Clubs: Creating special clubs or groups where ardent followers get additional perks and a closer connection to the brand.

20. Continuously Evolving Community Strategies

- Adapting to Change: Recognizing that communities evolve, and so should the strategies to engage them.
- Staying Updated: Regularly revisiting and revising community-building tactics based on feedback, trends, and platform changes.

Concluding Thoughts for Chapter 6

A thriving community on Pinterest is a testament to a brand's commitment to its audience. It's a space where mutual respect, shared values, and genuine interactions culminate in strong brand loyalty. With thoughtful strategies and a keen understanding of your audience's needs and desires, you can cultivate a Pinterest community that's not just about numbers, but about meaningful connections that drive long-term growth and brand advocacy.

As we continue our deep dive into Pinterest, the subsequent chapters will elucidate more nuanced facets of the platform. From tapping into niche markets to ensuring sustained growth, every chapter will equip you with knowledge and tools for Pinterest mastery.

Chapter 7: Delving Deep into Pinterest Analytics: Driving Decisions with Data

The key to mastering any platform is to understand its analytics. Pinterest offers a plethora of insights that can guide content strategies, optimize engagement, and help brands tap into what truly resonates with their audience. This chapter will provide a comprehensive overview of Pinterest's analytics tools, illustrating how to extract meaningful data and utilize it for enhanced success.

1. Introduction to Pinterest Analytics
- The Power of Data: Why understanding analytics is crucial for success on Pinterest.
- Navigation Basics: A primer on accessing and navigating Pinterest's analytics dashboard.

2. Understanding the Key Metrics
- Impressions: Measuring how often your pins appear on a user's screen.
- Saves (Re-pins): Tracking how frequently your content is saved to other boards.
- Clicks: Gauging direct engagement with your pins and the resulting website traffic.
- Engagement Rate: Calculating the percentage of users who engaged with your pin after seeing it.

3. Audience Insights
- Demographics: Delving into the age, gender, location, and device preferences of your audience.
- Interests: Identifying the top categories and topics your audience engages with.
- Behaviors: Understanding when and how often your audience interacts with your content.

4. Evaluating Pin Performance
- Best Performing Pins: Identifying which pins drive the most engagement and traffic.
- Trends Over Time: Observing how pin performance fluctuates over days, weeks, or months.

- Video Pin Analytics: Diving into unique metrics for video content like play duration and replay frequency.

5. Analyzing Website Activity
- Website Link Clicks: Tracking the number of users directed to your website from Pinterest.
- Conversion Tracking: Setting up and monitoring actions taken on your site as a result of Pinterest traffic (e.g., purchases, sign-ups).
- Bounce Rate: Understanding the percentage of Pinterest-originated visitors who navigate away from your site after viewing only one page.

6. The Power of Story Pin Analytics
- Story Impressions: Measuring the visibility of your story pins.
- Story Engagement: Tracking saves, link clicks, and other interactions on your story content.
- Story Metrics vs. Regular Pin Metrics: Comparing and contrasting to optimize your content strategy.

7. Leveraging Competitor Analysis
- Identifying Key Competitors: Recognizing brands or profiles that share a similar audience or content theme.
- Benchmarking: Comparing your metrics against competitors to identify strengths and areas for improvement.
- Learning from the Best: Adopting effective strategies observed from top-performing competitors.

8. Tailoring Content Based on Insights
- Content Iteration: Using performance metrics to refine and adjust your content strategy.
- Experimentation: Regularly testing new content types, formats, or posting times and evaluating their performance.
- Feedback Loop: Incorporating audience feedback and insights into content creation.

9. Predictive Analytics and Future Trends
- Anticipating Trends: Using data to predict upcoming popular topics or themes on Pinterest.
- Preemptive Strategy Development: Crafting content in advance to align with anticipated trends.

- Staying Ahead of the Curve: Ensuring your brand remains relevant and ahead of competitors.

10. Making Data-Driven Decisions
- Strategic Planning: Basing future campaigns, promotions, or product launches on concrete data.
- Budgeting and ROI: Using analytics to determine where to allocate resources and evaluating the return on investment for Pinterest initiatives.
- Continuous Learning: Committing to regularly revisiting and updating knowledge on Pinterest analytics as the platform evolves.

11. The Role of UTM Parameters
- Tracking Precision: How to use UTM parameters to trace the exact origin of your website traffic from Pinterest.
- Campaign Specific Monitoring: Observing the performance of specific Pinterest campaigns or promotions using UTM tags.
- Integrating with Google Analytics: Combining Pinterest data with Google Analytics to gain a comprehensive understanding of user behavior post-click.

12. Audience Growth and Retention Metrics
- Follower Growth Rate: Tracking the increase of your followers over time and identifying growth trends.
- Retention Rate: Measuring the percentage of your followers who continue to engage with your content over a specific time period.
- Churn Rate: Identifying the number of followers who disengage or unfollow, and understanding potential reasons.

13. Seasonal Performance Insights
- Seasonal Trends: Recognizing the fluctuation of engagement based on seasons, holidays, or events.
- Tailored Content Strategy: Planning content in advance to leverage upcoming seasonal trends.
- Post-Season Analysis: Evaluating the performance post-season to draw lessons for future campaigns.

14. Advanced Analytics Tools and Integrations
- Third-Party Tools: Exploring tools outside of Pinterest that offer advanced analytics capabilities.

- Integration Benefits: Combining Pinterest data with other platforms for enhanced insights, such as merging Pinterest and e-commerce data.
- Data Visualization: Using tools to create visual reports that make complex data more digestible and actionable.

15. Ad Performance Analytics
- Promoted Pins Insights: Evaluating the performance of your paid promotions on Pinterest.
- ROI on Ad Spend: Calculating the returns on your advertising investments.
- Ad Iteration: Adjusting and refining ad strategies based on performance data.

16. Engagement Depth: Beyond the Surface Metrics
- Depth of Interaction: Distinguishing between passive engagement (e.g., scrolling past) and active engagement (e.g., saving, clicking).
- Content Resonance: Identifying which content themes or formats evoke deeper connections with the audience.

17. Feedback Analytics: Listening to Your Audience
- Comments and Messages: Analyzing feedback received directly from your Pinterest followers.
- Sentiment Analysis: Using tools to gauge the overall sentiment of comments and mentions related to your brand on Pinterest.

18. Optimizing for Mobile vs. Desktop Users
- Device-Specific Insights: Understanding how user behavior differs between mobile and desktop.
- Tailored Content: Adjusting pin dimensions, content format, and call-to-actions based on device preferences.

19. Setting and Tracking KPIs (Key Performance Indicators)
- Defining Success: Establishing clear KPIs based on your brand's goals on Pinterest.
- Regular Monitoring: Ensuring you're on track to meet or exceed these indicators and adjusting strategies as needed.

20. Continuous Education and Adaptation

- Staying Updated: Regularly checking in on Pinterest's evolving analytics offerings and updates.
- Feedback Loop: Continually revising strategies based on new data insights and platform changes.

Concluding Thoughts for Chapter 7

Understanding and leveraging analytics is akin to having a roadmap for success on Pinterest. It illuminates the path, highlights potential pitfalls, and provides the tools to navigate challenges. By adopting a data-driven approach, brands can ensure that their Pinterest strategy is not only effective but also continuously evolving to meet the changing demands of the platform and its users.

In our subsequent chapters, we'll delve deeper into monetization strategies, collaborations, and the art of storytelling on Pinterest, ensuring that your brand not only thrives but also leads in this dynamic digital landscape.

Chapter 8: Advanced Monetization Strategies: Turning Pins into Profits

Pinterest is more than just a platform for sharing inspirational content; it's a hub for businesses and creators to drive sales and generate income. To truly harness the power of Pinterest for monetization, one must go beyond the basics. This chapter delves into advanced strategies to maximize profitability and turn your Pinterest endeavors into a thriving revenue stream.

1. Introduction to Advanced Monetization
- Beyond the Basics: Understanding the untapped potential of Pinterest for generating income.
- Aligning with Platform Dynamics: Recognizing the unique characteristics of Pinterest that make it a powerful platform for monetization.

2. Rich Pins and Enhanced Product Information
- The Power of Rich Pins: How additional information, like real-time pricing and stock availability, can drive sales.
- Setting Up Rich Pins: A step-by-step guide to integrating your website's metadata with Pinterest.

3. Diversifying Affiliate Marketing Strategies
- Multiple Affiliate Networks: Engaging with various networks to expand product range and commission opportunities.
- Tailored Pin Descriptions: Crafting descriptions that naturally incorporate affiliate links without appearing overly promotional.

4. Introducing New Product Launches
- Teaser Campaigns: Using Pinterest to generate buzz and anticipation for upcoming products.
- Exclusive Pinterest Discounts: Offering special discounts for followers to incentivize purchases.

5. Collaborative Boards for Increased Exposure
- Joining Niche Boards: Collaborating on boards with other pinners in your niche to tap into their audience.
- Creating Group Boards: Inviting influencers and industry leaders to co-curate, amplifying reach.

6. Shoppable Pins: Seamless Shopping Experiences
- Instant Purchasing: Allowing users to buy products directly from pins without navigating away.
- Optimizing for Conversions: Ensuring your shoppable pins have high-quality images, detailed descriptions, and clear pricing.

7. Sponsored Content and Brand Partnerships
- Identifying Suitable Brands: Collaborating with brands that align with your Pinterest theme and audience.
- Delivering Authentic Promotions: Crafting sponsored pins that resonate with your followers while fulfilling partnership agreements.

8. Hosting Paid Workshops and Webinars
- Skill Sharing: Leveraging Pinterest's audience to promote and sell educational content.
- Engaging Visuals: Creating captivating pins to advertise your workshops or webinars.

9. Selling Digital Products and Downloads
- Printables, E-Books, and Courses: Using Pinterest to promote and distribute digital goods.
- Exclusive Preview Pins: Offering snippets or samples to entice potential buyers.

10. Incorporating Video for Product Showcases
- Video Pins: Demonstrating product use or revealing behind-the-scenes content to engage users.
- CTAs in Video Content: Embedding strong call-to-actions to drive sales or sign-ups.

11. Subscription-Based Models and Memberships
- Exclusive Content: Promoting premium, subscribers-only content on Pinterest.
- Recurring Revenue: Harnessing the power of subscription models for consistent income.

12. Engaging with Trend Predictions
- Staying Ahead of the Curve: Utilizing Pinterest's trend predictions to stock up or create relevant products.
- Capitalizing on Viral Trends: Quickly adapting to and monetizing from fast-spreading trends.

13. Optimizing for Mobile Shoppers
- Mobile-Friendly Landing Pages: Ensuring that your linked websites or shops are optimized for mobile users.
- Swift Loading Times: Recognizing the importance of quick load times to retain potential customers.

14. Retargeting Strategies for Abandoned Carts
- Retargeting Pins: Creating pins specifically aimed at users who've previously shown interest but didn't finalize a purchase.
- Discounts and Incentives: Offering special deals to lure back potential customers.

15. A/B Testing for Monetization Strategies
- Experimenting with Variations: Testing different pin designs, descriptions, or CTAs to determine what drives the best results.
- Analyzing and Adapting: Using the insights from tests to refine and optimize monetization techniques.

16. Sponsored Pins: Paid Advertising with a Twist
- Why Sponsored Pins: Understanding the benefits and potential ROI from using Pinterest's native advertising.
- Crafting Effective Sponsored Pins: Techniques for designing pins that not only capture attention but also lead to conversions.

17. Expanding Reach through Promoted Video Pins

- Visual Storytelling: The power of video in conveying a product's benefits, usage, and story.
- Budgeting and Bidding: Deciding on a budget for video promotions and understanding Pinterest's bidding system.

18. Harnessing the Power of Story Pins for Monetization
- Sequential Storytelling: Building a narrative around your product or service to engage viewers progressively.
- Direct and Indirect Monetization with Stories: Using stories for both immediate sales and longer-term brand-building.

19. Pinterest Shop: Building Your Storefront on Pinterest
- Setting Up: Walkthrough of creating your very own Pinterest Shop.
- Optimizing Product Listings: Best practices for product descriptions, images, and categorization within the Pinterest Shop environment.

20. Engaging with Pinterest Communities for Business Growth
- Pinterest Communities: Leveraging these groups to promote products, gain feedback, and engage with a loyal customer base.
- User-Generated Content: Encouraging satisfied customers to share their own pins featuring your products, further increasing reach and authenticity.

21. Affiliate Marketing: Advanced Tips
- Deep Linking: Directing potential customers straight to the product page rather than a homepage, increasing the chances of conversion.
- Disclosure Practices: Staying transparent and compliant with Pinterest's guidelines on affiliate promotions.

22. Diversifying Revenue Streams
- Multiple Monetization Models: Combining direct sales, affiliate marketing, sponsored content, and other strategies for a robust income model.
- Risk Management: Safeguarding against changes in Pinterest algorithms, policies, or market trends by not putting all your eggs in one basket.

23. Continuous Monitoring and Adaptation

- Regular Analytics Check-ins: Evaluating the performance of your monetization strategies and adapting based on data.
- Staying Updated: Keeping abreast of Pinterest's evolving features, tools, and monetization opportunities.

24. Collaboration with Influencers for Enhanced Reach
- Finding the Right Fit: Identifying influencers whose audience aligns with your target demographic.
- Win-Win Partnerships: Structuring collaborations that benefit both the brand and the influencer.

25. Utilizing Third-Party Tools for Sales Integration
- E-commerce Integrations: Tools and plugins that seamlessly integrate your online store with Pinterest, facilitating direct sales.
- Inventory Management: Systems that help in real-time stock updates on Pinterest, ensuring customers always have accurate information.

Concluding Thoughts for Chapter 8

Monetizing Pinterest effectively requires a blend of creativity, strategy, and adaptability. With the multitude of tools and features that the platform offers, brands and creators are equipped with what they need to generate a substantial income. The key lies in understanding the nuances of these features, staying updated with platform changes, and always keeping the end-user's experience at the forefront of all strategies.

By mastering these advanced monetization techniques and continuously iterating based on feedback and analytics, you'll not only drive revenue but also build a loyal and engaged Pinterest community around your brand or products.

As we move forward, we'll delve deeper into leveraging collaborations on Pinterest, understanding the intricacies of teaming up with influencers, other brands, and harnessing user-generated content to bolster your brand's presence and profitability.

Chapter 9: Harnessing Collaborations and Partnerships on Pinterest

Pinterest, with its community-driven focus, offers ample opportunities for brands and creators to harness the power of collaborations. Whether it's teaming up with influencers, forming alliances with complementary brands, or fostering user-generated content, collaborations can be a game-changer. This chapter will guide you through the intricacies of these partnerships and how to maximize their potential for growth and engagement.

1. Introduction to Collaborative Power on Pinterest
- The Collaborative Advantage: Understanding why collaborations are essential for Pinterest growth.
- Diverse Partnership Opportunities: Exploring the various avenues of collaborations available on Pinterest.

2. Influencer Collaborations: Finding Your Brand Ambassadors
- Identifying the Right Influencers: Techniques for finding influencers that align with your brand values and target audience.
- Crafting a Win-Win Agreement: Establishing clear terms that benefit both parties, ensuring successful and smooth collaboration.

3. Group Boards: The Power of Collective Curation
- Setting Up a Group Board: Guidelines for creating and managing a collaborative board.
- Engaging the Right Collaborators: Inviting relevant, active, and influential Pinterest users to contribute.

4. Co-Hosting Pinterest Contests and Giveaways
- Planning a Collaborative Contest: Steps to set up a joint contest that boosts engagement and offers value to participants.
- Promotion and Execution: Ensuring maximum visibility and seamless execution of the contest.

5. Collaborating with Complementary Brands

- Finding Synergistic Partners: Identifying brands that offer complementary products or services to yours.
- Joint Marketing Campaigns: Crafting campaigns that highlight the strengths of both brands.

6. User-Generated Content (UGC): Authentic Brand Advocacy
- Encouraging UGC: Strategies to motivate your audience to create content that features your products or services.
- Showcasing and Rewarding: Ways to feature UGC on your boards and offer incentives for quality content creation.

7. Pinterest Takeovers: Guest Curators and Influencers
- Planning a Takeover: Allowing an influencer or industry expert to curate your Pinterest content for a set period.
- Promotion and Monitoring: Maximizing the visibility of the takeover and ensuring alignment with brand guidelines.

8. Webinars and Workshops: Teaming Up for Education
- Identifying Topics and Experts: Finding relevant subject matter and collaborating with experts for educational sessions.
- Promotion on Pinterest: Techniques to advertise and draw attendees via Pinterest.

9. Collaborative Ad Campaigns for Enhanced Reach
- Joint Advertising Ventures: Pooling resources with complementary brands to run more extensive ad campaigns on Pinterest.
- Shared Benefits and Responsibilities: Distributing the campaign's outcomes and duties equitably between collaborating parties.

10. Partnership Metrics: Measuring the Success of Collaborations
- Key Performance Indicators (KPIs): Establishing metrics to evaluate the effectiveness of collaborations.
- Continuous Feedback and Adaptation: Using data to refine and optimize collaborative strategies.

11. Navigating Challenges in Collaborations
- Common Pitfalls: Recognizing and avoiding typical issues in Pinterest collaborations.

- Conflict Resolution: Addressing and resolving disagreements or misalignments that arise during collaborations.

12. Leveraging Collaborations for Monetization
- Affiliate Partnerships: Promoting each other's products for a commission on sales.
- Joint Product Launches: Collaborating on product development and leveraging each other's audiences for sales.

13. Building Long-Term Relationships with Collaborators
- Sustaining Momentum: Tips for maintaining the energy and synergy of initial collaborations for long-term benefits.
- Regular Check-ins: The importance of consistent communication with collaborators to ensure alignment and address concerns.

14. Expanding Collaborations Beyond Pinterest
- Cross-Platform Strategies: Leveraging collaborative success on Pinterest to form partnerships on other social media platforms and websites.
- Integrated Marketing Campaigns: Combining resources for larger, multi-channel campaigns that capitalize on the strengths of both partners.

15. Case Studies: Successful Collaborations on Pinterest
- Analysis of Top Collaborative Campaigns: A deep dive into some of the most impactful and innovative partnership efforts on Pinterest, drawing lessons and inspiration.
- Keys to Their Success: Identifying the strategies, tactics, and choices that made certain collaborations stand out.

16. Legal and Ethical Considerations in Collaborations
- Contracts and Agreements: The importance of clearly documented terms to avoid misunderstandings and protect all parties involved.
- Disclosure Requirements: Understanding the need to maintain transparency with the audience about promotional and sponsored content.

17. Feedback Loops: Ensuring Continuous Improvement
- Gathering Feedback: Techniques for collecting feedback from both collaborators and the audience.

• Iterative Refinement: Using feedback to refine collaboration strategies, ensuring they remain effective and relevant.

18. Celebrating Collaborative Wins

• Showcasing Success Stories: Publicly acknowledging and celebrating successful partnerships to boost morale and motivate future collaborations.

• Gratitude and Acknowledgment: The importance of expressing appreciation to collaborators, further cementing strong working relationships.

19. Leveraging Technology for Seamless Collaborations

• Collaboration Tools: Recommendations for tools and software that facilitate easy communication, planning, and execution of joint campaigns.

• Integration with Pinterest: Ensuring that tech tools work seamlessly with Pinterest's interface and features.

20. Re-evaluating and Ending Collaborations

• Signs It's Time to Move On: Recognizing when a collaboration is no longer beneficial or aligned with brand goals.

• Graceful Exits: Tips for ending partnerships amicably, preserving relationships, and maintaining brand reputation.

Concluding Thoughts for Chapter 9

The dynamic nature of Pinterest, coupled with its visually rich and community-oriented environment, makes it an ideal platform for collaborations. Whether you're a solo creator, an emerging brand, or an established business, harnessing the power of partnerships can drastically amplify your reach, influence, and revenue on Pinterest.

Remember, collaborations aren't just about increasing numbers or sales. They're about building relationships, learning from others, and offering mutual value. Approach each partnership with an open mind, clear communication, and a shared vision, and you'll find yourself in a world filled with opportunities and growth on Pinterest.

Next, we delve deeper into understanding the psychology of Pinterest users. What motivates them to pin, save, or purchase? How can you align your strategies with their desires and pain points? Chapter 10 will unravel these mysteries, equipping you with insights to craft more impactful Pinterest campaigns.

Chapter 10: Decoding the Pinterest User: Psychology, Motivations, and Behaviors

To truly succeed on Pinterest, it's essential to understand the people behind the pins. By delving deep into the psyche of Pinterest users, brands and creators can tailor their content and strategies to resonate more profoundly with their audience. This chapter aims to demystify the motivations, behaviors, and preferences of Pinterest users, allowing you to connect and engage with them on a deeper level.

1. Introduction: The Unique World of Pinterest Users
   • Distinguishing Characteristics: Understanding what sets Pinterest users apart from users of other social platforms.
   • The Pinterest Mindset: A look into the primary motivations that drive users to the platform.

2. The Pinterest Journey: From Inspiration to Action
   • Seeking Inspiration: Exploring the mindset of users looking for ideas and inspirations.
   • The Decision-Making Process: How pins influence users' choices, from simple DIY projects to significant life decisions.

3. The Emotional Connection: Why Users Love Pinterest
   • Visual Storytelling: The power of images in evoking emotions and creating connections.
   • Dreams and Aspirations: How Pinterest acts as a canvas for users to envision their ideal lives.

4. Categories That Resonate: Popular Niches on Pinterest
   • Home and Decor: The allure of designing one's living space.
   • Fashion and Beauty: Personal expression and staying updated with trends.
   • DIY and Crafts: The joy of creation and personalization.

5. The Purchase Behavior: From Browsing to Buying
- Trust in Pinterest: Why users are more likely to trust product recommendations on Pinterest compared to other platforms.
- The Role of Authentic Reviews and UGC: How user-generated content influences purchasing decisions.

6. Pinning Patterns: Understanding User Engagement
- Frequent Pinners: Habits and behaviors of users who pin content regularly.
- Seasonal Trends: How pinning behavior changes with holidays, seasons, and special events.

7. The Role of Community: Engaging with Others on Pinterest
- Group Boards and Collaboration: The importance of collective curation and shared interests.
- Community Engagement: How interactions on Pinterest foster a sense of belonging.

8. Personalized Experience: The Allure of Tailored Content
- Algorithm Insights: How Pinterest's algorithm curates content based on user behavior and preferences.
- The Joy of Discovery: The balance between seeking specific content and stumbling upon new inspirations.

9. Challenges and Pain Points of Pinterest Users
- Information Overload: Navigating the vast sea of pins and boards.
- Authenticity Concerns: Distinguishing genuine recommendations from sponsored content.

10. Adapting to Evolving User Expectations
- Staying Updated with Trends: The importance of keeping content fresh and relevant.
- Feedback and Adaptation: Regularly seeking feedback and making necessary adjustments to strategies.

11. Building Trust and Credibility with Users
- Transparency in Promotions: Clearly marking sponsored content and ads.
- Quality Over Quantity: The importance of curating high-quality, relevant pins over sheer volume.

12. Psychological Triggers: Crafting Pins that Compel Action
- Using Color Psychology: How different colors can evoke specific emotions and actions.

- Powerful Imagery and Copy: Combining visuals with compelling text to make pins irresistible.

13. The Role of Storytelling in User Engagement
- Narrative-driven Pins: The power of a story in making content more relatable and memorable.
- User Stories: Highlighting real-life experiences and testimonials to foster trust and relatability.

14. Understanding Different User Segments
- Demographic Insights: How age, gender, and location can influence Pinterest behavior and preferences.
- Lifestyle Segmentation: Catering to different user groups, from travelers and foodies to parents and fitness enthusiasts.

15. Bridging the Gap: Connecting Offline and Online Experiences
- Physical Events and Pinterest: How offline events, like workshops or product launches, can be enhanced with Pinterest engagement.
- Virtual Reality and Augmented Reality: Exploring the future of immersive Pinterest experiences.

16. Feedback Mechanisms: Listening to the Voice of the User
- Surveys and Polls: Actively seeking user feedback to understand their evolving needs and preferences.
- Comments and Messages: Valuable insights from direct user interactions on the platform.

17. Future Trends: Predicting Evolving User Behavior
- Emerging Interests: Staying ahead of the curve by identifying and capitalizing on new user interests and trends.
- Adapting to Technological Advancements: How innovations like AI and AR might shape user behavior on Pinterest.

18. User Retention Strategies: Keeping the Pinterest Audience Engaged
- Refreshed Content: Regularly updating boards and pins to cater to changing user interests.
- Interactive Pins: Using polls, quizzes, and other engagement tools to keep the audience involved.

19. Authenticity vs. Aesthetics: Striking the Right Balance

- Genuine Content: The importance of staying true to your brand voice and values.
- Visual Appeal: Ensuring pins are aesthetically pleasing without compromising on authenticity.

20. Understanding International Pinterest Users

- Cultural Sensitivities: Catering to a global audience while being mindful of cultural nuances.
- Localized Content: Adapting pins and boards to cater to specific geographical regions.

Concluding Thoughts for Chapter 10

Truly understanding Pinterest users is a blend of art and science. It involves studying user behavior, keeping up with emerging trends, and most importantly, fostering genuine human connections. By creating content that resonates emotionally, aligns with user aspirations, and addresses specific pain points, you can craft a Pinterest strategy that not only boosts metrics but also builds meaningful relationships. In the next chapter, we will shift our focus to advanced Pinterest strategies. From leveraging Pinterest analytics to exploring growth hacks, we'll delve into techniques that can give you a competitive edge on the platform. Whether you're a seasoned pinner or just getting started, these insights will equip you with tools to propel your Pinterest success to new heights.

Chapter 11: Advanced Pinterest Strategies: Leveraging Analytics, Growth Hacks, and More

For those looking to maximize their impact on Pinterest, understanding and utilizing advanced strategies is key. This chapter will delve deep into sophisticated techniques, analytics-driven decision-making, and innovative growth hacks that can set you apart in the crowded Pinterest landscape.

1. Introduction: Beyond the Basics

- Rising Above the Noise: The importance of standing out in an ever-evolving platform.

- The Power of Data: Utilizing Pinterest analytics to drive decision-making.

2. Deep Dive into Pinterest Analytics
- Key Metrics to Track: Understanding metrics like impressions, saves, link clicks, and more.
- Interpreting Data: Translating numbers into actionable insights for content creation and strategy adjustment.

3. A/B Testing on Pinterest
- Why Test?: The significance of experimentation in determining what resonates with your audience.
- Conducting Effective Tests: Best practices for setting up, running, and analyzing A/B tests on your pins.

4. Exploring Pinterest SEO
- Keyword Research: Identifying high-performing keywords tailored to your niche.
- Optimizing Pins for Search: Implementing keywords in pin titles, descriptions, and even image alt texts.

5. Tailwind and Pinterest: A Powerful Duo
- Introduction to Tailwind: Overview of this popular Pinterest scheduling and analytics tool.
- Maximizing Tailwind's Features: Harnessing the power of Tailwind Tribes, SmartLoop, and more.

6. The Art of Pin Design
- Visual Hierarchy: Ensuring the most critical elements of your pin capture attention.
- Branding Consistency: Incorporating brand colors, logos, and fonts for instant recognition.

7. Crafting Irresistible Pin Descriptions
- Keyword-Rich Descriptions: Balancing SEO with engaging storytelling.
- Call-to-Action (CTA) Inclusion: Encouraging users to take specific actions, from clicking through to leaving comments.

8. Diversifying Content: Videos, Carousel Pins, and Story Pins
- Leveraging Video Pins: Best practices for creating and optimizing video content on Pinterest.
- Maximizing Carousel and Story Pins: Using multi-image pins to tell richer stories and showcase products.

9. Pinterest Advertising: Advanced Techniques
- Setting Clear Campaign Goals: Determining what you want to achieve, be it brand awareness, traffic, or conversions.
- Targeting and Retargeting: Refining audience segments for more effective ad delivery.

10. Engaging with the Pinterest Community
- Joining and Creating Group Boards: Collaborative pinning as a strategy for increased reach and engagement.
- Engaging Authentically: Building genuine connections through comments, messages, and more.

11. Expanding Reach through Repurposing Content
- From Blog to Pin: Turning blog content into multiple pins.
- Cross-Promotion: Leveraging content from other platforms to create fresh pins.

12. Staying Updated with Pinterest Trends
- Using Pinterest Trends Tool: Gaining insights into rising search terms and popular topics.
- Seasonal Content Planning: Aligning content strategy with holidays, seasons, and events.

13. Scheduled Pinning: Maximizing Impact with Timing
- Best Times to Pin: Identifying peak engagement hours for your target audience.
- Frequency and Consistency: Determining the ideal number of daily pins and maintaining a regular posting schedule.

14. Collaborations and Partnerships on Pinterest
- Influencer Collaborations: Leveraging the reach and credibility of Pinterest influencers in your niche.
- Brand Partnerships: Engaging in joint campaigns or board collaborations to expand your reach.

15. The Power of Rich Pins
- Types of Rich Pins: Exploring Article, Product, Recipe, and App Pins.
- Setting Up and Optimizing Rich Pins: Harnessing additional metadata to make your pins more informative and actionable.

16. Mobile Optimization: Catering to the On-the-Go Pinner

- Responsive Pin Design: Ensuring pins look appealing across desktop, tablet, and mobile devices.
- Mobile-Friendly Landing Pages: Providing seamless experiences for users clicking through from pins.

17. Converting Pinners to Subscribers
- Lead Magnets: Offering valuable freebies, like eBooks or templates, to entice users to subscribe to your mailing list.
- Seamless Sign-Up Processes: Integrating user-friendly sign-up forms and ensuring GDPR compliance.

18. Analyzing Competitors on Pinterest
- Keeping an Eye on the Competition: Understanding what other players in your niche are doing right (or wrong).
- Learning and Adapting: Drawing inspiration without directly copying; forging your unique path.

19. User-Generated Content (UGC): A Goldmine for Engagement
- Encouraging UGC: Motivating your followers to create and share content related to your brand or products.
- Showcasing UGC: Featuring user-created pins on your boards, in ads, or even on other platforms.

20. Continuous Learning: Staying Updated with Pinterest's Evolving Landscape
- Attending Webinars and Workshops: Participating in educational events hosted by Pinterest or industry experts.
- Subscribing to Pinterest Blogs and Newsletters: Keeping a finger on the pulse of platform updates, trends, and best practices.

Concluding Thoughts for Chapter 11

Mastering advanced Pinterest strategies is a continuous journey of exploration, testing, and adaptation. As the platform evolves, so should your tactics. By staying informed, being flexible, and focusing on genuine user engagement, you can leverage Pinterest's full potential, driving both growth and meaningful interactions. Your Pinterest success will be defined not just by numbers but by the quality of connections you forge and the inspiration you provide to your audience.

In our subsequent chapter, we will turn our focus towards troubleshooting common challenges on Pinterest. From deciphering sudden drops in engagement to understanding and adapting to algorithm changes, we'll equip you with the knowledge and tools to navigate the highs and lows of your Pinterest journey with confidence.

Chapter 12: Troubleshooting Common Challenges on Pinterest

No platform is without its quirks and challenges, and Pinterest is no exception. Whether you're facing a sudden dip in engagement, perplexed by Pinterest's algorithm, or struggling with creating standout content, this chapter will equip you with strategies to navigate common hurdles with grace and efficacy.

1. Introduction: Navigating the Pinterest Puzzle
   • Accepting the Inevitable: Recognizing that challenges are a part of any digital journey.
   • The Power of Resilience: Emphasizing the importance of persistence and adaptability.

2. Addressing Dips in Engagement
   • Analyzing Potential Causes: From content saturation to algorithm changes, understanding potential reasons for decreased engagement.
   • Strategies for Revival: Refreshing content, experimenting with new formats, and re-engaging dormant followers.

3. Decoding the Pinterest Algorithm
   • Understanding the Basics: What does the algorithm prioritize, and how does it affect content visibility?
   • Adapting to Algorithm Shifts: Keeping content relevant, engaging, and in line with Pinterest's evolving criteria.

4. Overcoming Content Fatigue
   • Signs of Stagnation: Recognizing when your content starts to feel repetitive or lacks freshness.

- Breathing New Life: Diversifying pin formats, exploring new topics, and seeking inspiration from global trends.

5. Dealing with Copyright Issues
- Staying Informed: Understanding Pinterest's copyright policies and best practices.
- Proactive Measures: Using original content, sourcing images responsibly, and addressing copyright claims.

6. Maximizing Visibility in a Sea of Pins
- Enhancing Discoverability: Implementing advanced SEO strategies and staying active in community boards.
- Paid Promotions: Considering sponsored pins to boost visibility and reach.

7. Challenges in Pinterest Advertising
- Common Hurdles: Addressing issues like low click-through rates, high costs, and ad disapprovals.
- Optimizing Ad Performance: A/B testing, refining target audiences, and tweaking ad creatives.

8. Navigating Negative Feedback and Comments
- Constructive vs. Destructive Criticism: Identifying genuine feedback versus trolling.
- Handling Criticism Gracefully: Addressing concerns, moderating comments, and maintaining brand integrity.

9. Maintaining Authenticity Amidst Commercial Goals
- Balancing Act: Striking a balance between genuine content and promotional pins.
- Prioritizing Value: Ensuring that every pin, even promotional ones, offers value to the audience.

10. Evolving with Pinterest's Feature Updates
- Staying Updated: Keeping abreast of new features and platform changes.
- Adaptation Strategies: Seamlessly integrating new features into your existing Pinterest strategy.

11. Troubleshooting Technical Glitches
- Common Technical Issues: Addressing problems like pin upload failures, broken links, and account issues.
- Reaching Out: Utilizing Pinterest's support resources and community forums for assistance.

12. Addressing Audience Segmentation and Personalization

- The Importance of Targeting: Recognizing that not all pinners are created equal.
- Tailoring Content to Specific Audiences: Using analytics to segment your audience and personalizing content to resonate with each group.

13. Managing Time and Consistency
- Time Management Woes: The challenge of constantly creating, pinning, and engaging.
- Automating Processes: Leveraging tools like Tailwind to schedule pins and maintain a consistent presence.

14. Scaling Your Pinterest Efforts
- Growing Pains: As your account grows, so do the challenges related to content creation, engagement, and analysis.
- Effective Scaling Strategies: Building a team, outsourcing certain tasks, or using advanced management tools.

15. Avoiding Content Burnout
- The Creativity Conundrum: How to stay inspired and keep producing fresh content.
- Seeking External Inspiration: Collaborating with other pinners, joining creative challenges, or simply taking a break to rejuvenate.

16. Competing with Larger Brands and Influencers
- David vs. Goliath: The challenges smaller accounts face in a space dominated by big names.
- Carving Your Unique Niche: Focusing on your unique selling proposition (USP) and connecting deeply with a specific audience segment.

17. Adapting to Mobile-First Users
- The Mobile Majority: With many users accessing Pinterest via mobile, how do you optimize for smaller screens?
- Responsive Design Principles: Ensuring pins and landing pages are mobile-friendly.

18. Understanding International Audiences
- Global Appeal: As Pinterest expands globally, how can you cater to an international audience?

- Localization Strategies: Translating content, understanding cultural nuances, and engaging with local trends.

19. Transitioning Followers to Other Platforms
- Beyond Pinterest: Leveraging your Pinterest success to grow on other platforms.
- Seamless Transitions: Strategies to encourage pinners to follow you on Instagram, subscribe on YouTube, or join your email list.

20. Reevaluating and Pivoting Strategies
- Changing Tides: What to do when a once-successful strategy is no longer effective?
- Embracing Change: Continuously assessing, learning, and being willing to change direction when needed.

Concluding Thoughts for Chapter 12

Addressing challenges on Pinterest is not just about troubleshooting problems as they arise, but also anticipating potential hurdles and being prepared with solutions. By being proactive, staying informed, and maintaining a flexible approach, you can navigate the ever-evolving landscape of Pinterest with confidence. Embrace challenges as they come, for they offer valuable lessons and opportunities to refine your strategies.

In the next chapter, we will focus on the future. As the digital world rapidly evolves, so does Pinterest. We'll explore how to anticipate emerging trends, predict user behavior shifts, and position yourself as a pioneer in the Pinterest space. Success on the platform is not just about reacting to the present but also preparing for what's next.

Chapter 13: Predicting the Future: Anticipating Pinterest Trends and Staying Ahead

Staying ahead in the digital landscape requires foresight. While the present is essential, the future is where the next wave of opportunities lies. In this chapter, we'll explore the art and science of predicting Pinterest's trajectory, preparing for emerging trends, and ensuring that you're always one step ahead of the curve.

1. Introduction: The Ever-Evolving World of Pinterest
- The Digital Renaissance: Understanding that the online world, including Pinterest, is in a state of perpetual evolution.
- The Advantage of Foresight: Emphasizing the edge gained by those who can predict and prepare for upcoming trends.

2. Studying Pinterest's History to Predict its Future
- Patterns and Cycles: Recognizing recurring themes and shifts in user behavior over the years.
- Learning from the Past: Drawing parallels between past trends and potential future trajectories.

3. Monitoring Emerging Global Trends
- The Wider Digital Landscape: Understanding that Pinterest doesn't operate in a vacuum; global digital trends often influence platform-specific behaviors.
- Key Indicators: Watching out for shifts in related platforms, technological advancements, and broader cultural movements.

4. Engaging with Pinterest Communities
- The Power of Grassroots Insights: Recognizing that often, the most authentic predictors of trends are everyday users.
- Joining Pinterest Forums and Groups: Engaging with other pinners, attending Pinterest meetups, and participating in platform-specific discussions.

5. Utilizing Advanced Analytics Tools
- Beyond Basic Metrics: Exploring sophisticated tools that offer predictive analytics, sentiment analysis, and more.
- Interpreting Data with a Futuristic Lens: Translating current data patterns into potential future trends.

6. Observing Younger Demographics
- The Gen-Z Effect: Understanding that younger users often set the trends that later become mainstream.
- Engaging with and Observing Younger Pinners: Their behaviors, preferences, and pinning styles can provide valuable insights into Pinterest's future.

7. Anticipating Technological Advancements
- AR, VR, and Beyond: Exploring how emerging technologies might integrate with and influence Pinterest.
- Preparing for a Multi-dimensional Pinterest: Considering the possibilities of Pinterest entering the realms of augmented reality or virtual reality.

8. Staying Updated with Official Pinterest Announcements
- Direct from the Source: Keeping an eye on announcements, blog posts, and updates from Pinterest itself.
- Engaging with Beta Features: Trying out new features in their beta phase to get a jumpstart on upcoming trends.

9. Collaborating with Industry Thought Leaders
- Shared Wisdom: Engaging in conversations with digital marketing experts, Pinterest influencers, and industry insiders.
- Attending Webinars and Conferences: Staying updated with the latest in Pinterest strategy and predictions.

10. Diversifying and Experimenting
- Not Putting All Eggs in One Basket: Diversifying your Pinterest strategy to cater to multiple potential trends.
- The Power of Experimentation: Regularly trying out new content formats, strategies, and engagement techniques to see what resonates.

11. Recognizing Shifts in User Behavior and Preferences
- The Evolving User: Accepting that the Pinterest audience of today might not have the same preferences tomorrow.
- Conducting Regular Surveys: Engaging directly with your followers to understand their evolving needs and interests.

12. The Role of AI and Machine Learning
- The Technological Edge: Anticipating how Pinterest might leverage AI to enhance user experience and content discoverability.
- Staying Updated with AI Trends: Being aware of advancements in AI and considering how they might intersect with Pinterest's features.

13. Sustainability and Social Responsibility

- The Conscious Consumer: Recognizing the growing trend towards sustainability and ethical consumption.
- Aligning with Positive Movements: Creating and sharing content that resonates with these values, anticipating a larger shift in this direction on Pinterest.

14. Integrating Offline and Online Experiences
- The Physical-Digital Blur: Understanding the potential for Pinterest to bridge offline and online worlds, especially in retail and experiential sectors.
- Preparing for Hybrid Campaigns: Strategies that combine physical experiences with digital engagement on Pinterest.

15. The Rise of Niche Communities
- Specialized Interests: Predicting a move towards more niche boards and communities within Pinterest as users seek tailored experiences.
- Engaging Deeply with Specific Groups: Focusing on depth rather than breadth, catering to specific interests and communities.

16. Embracing New Content Formats
- Beyond Traditional Pins: Staying open to new formats like interactive pins, longer video content, or immersive storytelling experiences.
- Experimenting Proactively: Before a format becomes mainstream, familiarize yourself and be among the early adopters.

17. The Impact of Global Events
- The Bigger Picture: Understanding that global events, be it cultural festivals, socio-political changes, or economic shifts, influence trends on Pinterest.
- Staying Informed and Agile: Adapting your Pinterest strategy based on global happenings and user sentiments.

18. Building Authentic Connections
- Beyond Transactions: Predicting a shift from mere content consumption to building deeper, more authentic relationships with followers.
- Engagement Over Numbers: Focusing on genuine interactions, community building, and fostering trust.

Concluding Thoughts for Chapter 13

The future is a canvas painted with uncertainties, but it also holds immense potential. By proactively seeking insights, staying informed, and maintaining a flexible and adaptive approach, you can navigate the changing tides of Pinterest with confidence. The goal isn't just to adapt to future changes, but to be a trendsetter, leading the way and setting the pace for others to follow.

In the upcoming chapters, we will dive into broader aspects of digital marketing. We'll explore how to seamlessly integrate Pinterest into your overall online strategy, ensuring that your efforts on the platform complement and enhance your brand's presence across various digital touchpoints. This holistic approach will help amplify your online impact, creating a cohesive and powerful digital brand identity.

Chapter 14: Integrating Pinterest into Your Holistic Digital Marketing Strategy

In the digital realm, no platform is an island. To achieve maximum impact and ensure consistent branding, it's crucial to integrate Pinterest seamlessly into your broader digital marketing approach. This chapter will guide you through harmonizing your Pinterest efforts with other online platforms and strategies, creating a unified and powerful online presence.

1. Introduction: The Interconnected Digital Ecosystem
   • Synergy Over Isolation: The importance of viewing digital platforms as interconnected components of a larger system.
   • The Role of Pinterest: Positioning Pinterest within your overall digital marketing strategy and understanding its unique strengths.

2. Brand Consistency Across Platforms
   • Unified Brand Voice and Imagery: Ensuring that your brand's voice, imagery, and messaging are consistent on Pinterest and other platforms.

- Creating a Style Guide: Developing guidelines that ensure brand consistency across various digital touchpoints.

3. Cross-Promotion Strategies
- Leveraging Multiple Platforms: Using Pinterest to drive traffic to your blog, website, or other social media platforms, and vice versa.
- Effective Cross-Promotion Techniques: Strategies for guiding users from one platform to another without seeming pushy.

4. SEO and Pinterest
- Search Engine Harmony: Understanding the SEO benefits of Pinterest and how it can complement your website's search engine optimization.
- Optimizing Pins for Search: Techniques to enhance the discoverability of your Pinterest content on search engines.

5. Integrating Pinterest with Email Marketing
- Pin Newsletters: Incorporating Pinterest content into your email newsletters to drive engagement.
- Encouraging Email Subscriptions: Using Pinterest to grow your email list and nurture leads.

6. Pinterest and E-Commerce Integration
- Shop the Look: Leveraging Pinterest's shopping features to drive sales and connect with e-commerce platforms.
- Promoting Products on Pinterest: Effective strategies for showcasing products and driving traffic to e-commerce sites.

7. Collaborative Efforts with Influencers
- Unified Campaigns: Coordinating Pinterest campaigns with influencer collaborations on platforms like Instagram or YouTube.
- Amplifying Reach: Utilizing influencers' audiences to enhance your Pinterest content's reach and engagement.

8. Combining Pinterest with Content Marketing
- Driving Blog Traffic: Using Pinterest as a tool to boost blog readership and engagement.
- Promoting Long-Form Content: Strategies for using Pinterest to highlight eBooks, whitepapers, or detailed blog posts.

9. Pinterest Advertising and Paid Media Strategy
- Promoted Pins and Beyond: Integrating Pinterest's paid advertising options with your broader paid media campaigns.
- ROI and Budget Allocation: Deciding how much of your advertising budget to allocate to Pinterest based on performance metrics.

10. Utilizing Analytics for Holistic Insights
- Beyond Pinterest Analytics: Combining insights from Pinterest with analytics from your website, email marketing, and other platforms.
- Data-Driven Decisions: Making informed marketing choices based on comprehensive data analysis.

11. Engaging in Community Building
- Cross-Platform Engagement: Encouraging your Pinterest followers to join your communities on other platforms like Facebook groups or forums, and vice versa.
- Unified Community Values: Establishing and promoting the same set of values and community guidelines across all platforms to foster a sense of unity.

12. Integrating Pinterest with Video Marketing
- Video Pins and Beyond: The importance of video content on Pinterest and how it aligns with your broader video marketing strategy on platforms like YouTube or TikTok.
- Promoting Video Content: Strategies for drawing attention to your video content through Pinterest and ensuring consistency in messaging.

13. Synchronizing Seasonal Campaigns
- Coordinated Efforts: Ensuring that seasonal campaigns, whether it's for holidays, sales, or events, are synchronized across Pinterest and other platforms.
- Maximizing Seasonal Impact: Techniques to get the most out of these coordinated campaigns by leveraging the unique strengths of each platform.

14. Collaborating with Partners and Brands
- Cross-Platform Collaborations: Working with other brands or partners on joint campaigns that span Pinterest and other digital platforms.

• Shared Audiences: Techniques to mutually benefit from each brand's audience, enhancing reach and engagement.

15. Retargeting and Remarketing Efforts

• Unified Ad Strategy: Using insights from Pinterest engagements to inform retargeting campaigns on other platforms like Facebook or Google Ads.

• Maximizing Conversion: Techniques to ensure that users who engage with your brand on one platform are nudged towards conversion on another.

16. Incorporating User-Generated Content (UGC)

• UGC on Pinterest: Encouraging and showcasing user-generated content on Pinterest, and how it can be integrated into your UGC strategy on other platforms.

• Building Trust and Authenticity: Demonstrating how UGC can serve as social proof and build trust across your digital touchpoints.

17. Crisis Management and Brand Reputation

• Unified Response: Ensuring that in times of crisis, your brand's response and messaging are consistent across Pinterest and other platforms.

• Monitoring Brand Sentiment: Tools and techniques to keep a pulse on your brand's reputation across the digital landscape.

18. Continual Learning and Adaptation

• Staying Updated: The importance of keeping abreast with updates and changes on Pinterest and how they might affect your strategy on other platforms.

• Feedback Loops: Regularly gathering feedback from your audience across platforms to refine and optimize your strategies.

Concluding Thoughts for Chapter 14

Integrating Pinterest into a broader digital marketing framework is not just about simultaneous promotion. It's about creating a cohesive brand experience, no matter where your audience interacts with you. By approaching Pinterest as a piece of the larger digital puzzle, you can create synergies that amplify your brand's message, drive conversions, and foster deep and lasting connections with your audience.

As we move forward, our focus will shift to the final pieces of the puzzle, ensuring that your brand not only thrives on Pinterest but also evolves with it. From understanding algorithm changes to tapping into emerging features, the upcoming chapters will prepare you for sustained success on Pinterest and beyond.

Chapter 15: Building for Longevity: Ensuring Sustained Success on Pinterest

Achieving short-term success on Pinterest is one thing, but ensuring that success is sustained over the long term is another challenge altogether. In this chapter, we'll dive into strategies and practices that will help you build a lasting presence on Pinterest, ensuring your efforts stand the test of time.

1. Introduction: The Ever-Changing Digital Landscape
- The Nature of Digital Platforms: Recognizing that platforms, including Pinterest, evolve and change over time.
- Adapting vs. Reacting: The importance of proactive adaptation to ensure sustainable success.

2. Staying Updated with Platform Changes
- Regularly Reviewing Platform News: Subscribing to official channels and communities to stay informed about updates and changes on Pinterest.
- Testing New Features: Being among the first to experiment with and understand new Pinterest features.

3. Building a Loyal Community
- Beyond Numbers: Understanding that a smaller, engaged community is more valuable than a large, passive one.
- Community Engagement Strategies: Techniques for nurturing and maintaining strong relationships with your Pinterest followers.

4. Investing in Continuous Learning
- Staying Ahead of the Curve: The importance of continually updating your knowledge about Pinterest and digital marketing in general.

- Workshops and Courses: Seeking out educational opportunities to refine your Pinterest strategy.

5. Diversifying Content Types

- Avoiding Over-reliance: Ensuring that your Pinterest presence isn't solely dependent on one type of content or strategy.
- Experimentation: Regularly testing different content formats and approaches to see what resonates best with your audience.

6. Regular Performance Audits

- Reviewing Analytics: Periodically analyzing your Pinterest performance metrics to identify areas of strength and potential improvement.
- Setting Benchmarks: Establishing performance benchmarks to measure your progress and guide your strategy adjustments.

7. Future-Proofing Your Strategy

- Anticipating Changes: Predicting potential future shifts in user behavior or platform features and preparing for them in advance.
- Scalable Strategies: Implementing techniques and approaches that can grow and evolve with your brand.

8. Collaborating with Other Brands and Creators

- Mutually Beneficial Partnerships: Engaging in collaborations that bring fresh perspectives and approaches to your Pinterest strategy.
- Leveraging External Expertise: Working with Pinterest experts or agencies to refine and enhance your approach.

9. Emphasizing Authenticity and Transparency

- Building Trust: Recognizing the value of authenticity and transparency in fostering long-term loyalty among followers.
- Open Communication: Keeping your audience informed about changes, challenges, and successes related to your Pinterest activities.

10. Preparing for Potential Setbacks

- Crisis Management: Having plans in place for potential crises, such as PR issues, platform changes, or unexpected drops in engagement.
- Adaptive Strategies: Being ready to pivot your approach based on unforeseen challenges or changes.

11. Understanding the Importance of User Feedback
- Active Listening: Encouraging followers to share their opinions, preferences, and feedback about your Pinterest content.
- Feedback Mechanisms: Creating easy and accessible channels for users to voice their opinions, and being proactive in addressing concerns.

12. Staying Relevant in Your Niche
- Industry Trends: Regularly researching and updating yourself on the latest trends and shifts in your niche.
- Engaging with Thought Leaders: Networking and collaborating with influential figures in your industry to stay ahead.

13. Adapting to User Behavior Patterns
- Analyzing User Interactions: Deep diving into how users are interacting with your Pins and content to gain insights into their behavior and preferences.
- A/B Testing: Regularly experimenting with different content layouts, designs, and captions to determine what garners the most positive engagement.

14. Incorporating Technology Advancements
- Embracing New Tech: Staying informed about technological advancements that could be integrated into your Pinterest strategy, such as AR or VR.
- Optimizing for Mobile: Ensuring that all content is optimized for mobile viewing, given the predominant use of smartphones for accessing Pinterest.

15. Refreshing and Revamping Older Content
- Content Audits: Periodically reviewing and updating older Pins to ensure they remain relevant and accurate.
- Re-Purposing Content: Adapting and transforming successful older content into new formats or updating it with current trends.

16. Ensuring Sustainability in Collaborative Efforts

- Long-term Partnerships: Building lasting relationships with brands, influencers, or other collaborators that align with your brand values.
- Setting Clear Collaboration Guidelines: Establishing mutual expectations and goals for all collaborative projects.

17. Proactively Addressing Platform Limitations
- Staying Informed: Being aware of any limitations or restrictions on Pinterest and finding innovative ways to work within or around them.
- Feedback to Pinterest: Actively participating in user communities and providing constructive feedback to Pinterest to help shape its evolution.

18. Encouraging User Loyalty and Retention
- Loyalty Programs: Implementing strategies such as loyalty programs or exclusive content to incentivize followers to remain engaged.
- Consistent Value Proposition: Ensuring that you consistently deliver value to your followers, making them less likely to unfollow or disengage.

Concluding Thoughts for Chapter 15

Building a lasting presence on Pinterest requires a combination of adaptability, foresight, and deep understanding of both the platform and your audience. By continuously re-evaluating and refining your strategies, you ensure that your brand remains a staple in the ever-evolving Pinterest landscape. Long-term success is not just about reacting to the now, but also proactively planning for the future.

As we step into the next chapter, we will further delve into the ethical landscape of Pinterest. Emphasizing best practices and ethical considerations is paramount for any brand looking to not only succeed but also to leave a positive imprint in the digital realm.

Chapter 16: Measuring ROI on Pinterest: Understanding Your Impact

The ultimate success of any marketing effort hinges not just on achieving visibility or engagement but on realizing tangible returns on your investment. This chapter delves into how to effectively measure the ROI of your Pinterest strategies, ensuring you can assess the true impact of your efforts.

1. Introduction: The Importance of ROI in Digital Marketing
- Beyond Vanity Metrics: Recognizing the difference between surface-level metrics and those that directly tie to business outcomes.
- Investment Considerations: Understanding that ROI isn't just monetary; it can also involve time, resources, and effort.

2. Defining Clear Objectives
- Goal Setting: Establishing specific, measurable, achievable, relevant, and time-bound (SMART) goals for your Pinterest efforts.
- Aligning with Business Outcomes: Ensuring your Pinterest objectives align with broader business goals.

3. Key Metrics to Monitor on Pinterest
- Engagement Metrics: Analyzing likes, repins, comments, and click-through rates.
- Conversion Metrics: Tracking sales, sign-ups, or other desired actions resulting from Pinterest referrals.
- Reach and Visibility: Understanding impressions, viewership, and overall visibility of your pins.

4. Utilizing Pinterest Analytics
- Platform Overview: An introduction to the tools and insights available through Pinterest Analytics.
- Interpreting Data: Translating raw data into actionable insights.

5. Assigning Monetary Value to Pinterest Actions
- Customer Lifetime Value (CLV): Calculating the value of a Pinterest-acquired customer over their engagement lifespan with your brand.

- Cost Per Action (CPA): Understanding how much you're spending for each conversion achieved through Pinterest.

6. Tools and Platforms for Enhanced ROI Tracking
- Third-Party Analytics Tools: Introduction to tools outside of Pinterest that can provide deeper insights and tracking capabilities.
- Integration with Website Analytics: Bridging the gap between Pinterest actions and on-site behavior using platforms like Google Analytics.

7. Evaluating Time and Resource Investment
- Quantifying Time: Understanding the hours put into content creation, engagement, strategy planning, etc.
- Assessing Resource Costs: Considering costs like design tools, paid promotions, collaborations, and other expenses.

8. Adjusting Strategy Based on ROI Insights
- Continuous Learning: Using ROI evaluations to inform future Pinterest strategies.
- Testing and Optimization: Regularly revisiting and adjusting your approach based on ROI outcomes.

9. Benchmarking Against Industry Standards
- Industry Averages: Understanding average ROI metrics for your specific industry or niche.
- Competitor Analysis: Gauging your success in the context of competitors or similar brands on Pinterest.

10. The Intangible Benefits and ROI
- Brand Awareness and Reputation: Appreciating the value of increased brand visibility and positive reputation, even if not directly monetizable.
- Community Building: Recognizing the long-term ROI of fostering a loyal and engaged Pinterest community.

11. Quantifying the Impact of Collaborations and Partnerships
- Tracking Partnership Metrics: Utilizing UTM parameters and dedicated landing pages to monitor traffic and conversions from partnership efforts.
- Evaluating Partnership Value: Assessing not just the immediate returns but also long-term benefits like increased brand exposure and audience crossover.

12. The Challenge of Attribution in Multi-Channel Marketing
- • Understanding Multi-Touch Attribution: Recognizing that a user's journey might span multiple channels before conversion.
- • Attribution Models: Exploring different models like first-touch, last-touch, and linear attribution to more accurately assign value to Pinterest in the conversion pathway.

13. Seasonal Variations and ROI
- • Accounting for Seasonality: Recognizing that ROI might fluctuate based on seasonal trends, especially in industries like fashion, travel, or holidays.
- • Strategic Planning: Leveraging seasonality to optimize content planning and promotional strategies for peak periods.

14. Balancing Paid and Organic Strategies
- • Paid Promotions ROI: Monitoring the effectiveness of promoted pins or ads in driving desired actions.
- • Organic Growth Value: Understanding the long-term ROI benefits of organic engagement and community-building.

15. Future-Proofing: Predictive ROI Analysis
- • Using Historical Data: Leveraging past performance metrics to predict future ROI.
- • Scenario Planning: Creating various ROI predictions based on different strategic approaches or market conditions.

16. Challenges in ROI Measurement
- • Data Overlaps: Addressing potential double counting or discrepancies between Pinterest Analytics and third-party tools.
- • Changing Platform Algorithms: Adapting to Pinterest's evolving algorithms which can affect visibility and engagement.

17. Celebrating Successes and Learning from Shortcomings
- • Case Studies: Documenting particularly successful campaigns or strategies as case studies for future reference.
- • Feedback Loops: Encouraging team discussions to understand what worked, what didn't, and why.

Concluding Thoughts for Chapter 16
Accurately measuring ROI on Pinterest, or any platform, is a blend of art and science. While hard metrics provide the

backbone for evaluation, qualitative insights and contextual understanding often fill in the gaps. By developing a comprehensive approach to ROI analysis, brands can optimize their Pinterest strategies, ensuring they get the most value from their investments and efforts.

In our next chapter, we will delve into potential pitfalls and challenges that brands may encounter on Pinterest. From algorithm shifts to evolving user behaviors and platform updates, understanding these challenges – and how to adeptly navigate them – is crucial for sustained success.

Chapter 17: Navigating Challenges on Pinterest

Every platform comes with its unique set of challenges, and Pinterest is no exception. While it offers vast opportunities for brands and businesses, there are potential pitfalls that can disrupt a brand's momentum. This chapter will help you anticipate, understand, and effectively tackle these challenges.

1. Introduction: Embracing the Dynamic Nature of Digital Platforms
   • Constant Evolution: Recognizing that platforms like Pinterest are continuously evolving, leading to both opportunities and challenges.
   • Adaptability as a Key: Emphasizing the importance of staying agile and adaptable in the face of changing dynamics.

2. Algorithm Changes and Their Impact
   • Understanding Algorithm Shifts: An overview of how Pinterest's algorithm has changed over the years.
   • Adapting Content Strategy: Tweaking content based on algorithm preferences without losing brand authenticity.

3. The Challenge of Saturated Niches
   • Standing Out in the Crowd: Strategies to differentiate your brand in oversaturated niches.
   • Diversifying Content: Exploring various content formats and themes to attract a broader audience.

4. Handling Negative Feedback and Criticism

- Constructive vs. Destructive: Learning to differentiate between valid criticism and plain negativity.
- Crisis Management: Best practices for addressing controversies or widespread negative feedback.

5. Evolving User Behavior and Preferences
- Staying Updated: Keeping an ear to the ground to understand shifting user behaviors.
- Conducting Regular Surveys: Engaging directly with your audience to gain insights into their preferences.

6. The Intricacies of Global Audiences
- Cultural Sensitivities: Ensuring content is respectful and relatable to a global audience.
- Localizing Content: Adapting content to cater to specific regional or cultural audiences.

7. Competition and Copycats
- Dealing with Imitators: Addressing those who might copy your content or style.
- Staying Ahead of the Curve: Continually innovating to remain unique and differentiated.

8. Technical Issues and Glitches
- Platform Bugs: Addressing occasional technical hiccups on Pinterest.
- Backup Plans: Having a plan in place for when technical issues disrupt your scheduled posts or campaigns.

9. Changes in Monetization Policies
- Staying Updated: Regularly reviewing Pinterest's monetization guidelines to ensure compliance.
- Diversifying Revenue Streams: Not relying solely on one method of monetization.

10. Navigating the Balance of Organic vs. Paid Content
- Over-reliance on Paid Promotions: The risks associated with neglecting organic content.
- Budget Fluctuations: Adapting to changes in advertising budgets without losing audience engagement.

Concluding Thoughts for Chapter 17

Challenges on digital platforms are inevitable. However, with a proactive approach, keen awareness, and the willingness to adapt, brands can not only navigate these challenges but often turn them into opportunities for growth. The dynamic nature of platforms like Pinterest demands resilience and creativity from brands, ensuring they continue to engage their audience effectively, regardless of the hurdles they face.

The subsequent chapter will focus on the future of Pinterest marketing. We will explore emerging trends, technological advancements, and the evolving landscape of this platform. It's essential for brands to not only address present challenges but to also be prepared for future shifts in the digital marketing realm.

Chapter 18: The Future of Pinterest Marketing

As with any digital platform, Pinterest is ever-evolving, driven by technological advancements, changing user behaviors, and wider market dynamics. To stay ahead of the curve, it's essential to anticipate where Pinterest is headed and how these changes might affect your brand's marketing efforts.

1. Introduction: The Fluid Landscape of Digital Marketing
- Anticipating Trends: Recognizing that foresight is a competitive advantage in the rapidly changing digital world.
- Commitment to Evolution: Understanding that brands must evolve alongside platforms to remain relevant.

2. Pinterest's Vision: Platform Developments and Announcements
- Platform Announcements: Keeping abreast of official announcements from Pinterest regarding new features, tools, or shifts in focus.
- Technology Integrations: Exploring how Pinterest might integrate with emerging technologies, such as augmented reality or AI-driven personalized experiences.

3. The Rise of Video Content on Pinterest
- Video Pins: The increasing prominence of video pins and how brands can leverage them for deeper engagement.
- Interactive Content: Predicting a shift towards more immersive, interactive video formats.

4. E-commerce and Shopping Integration
- Shop the Look: The evolution of shoppable pins and how brands can utilize them to drive direct sales.

- Integration with E-commerce Platforms: Anticipating deeper integrations with platforms like Shopify or WooCommerce for a seamless shopping experience.

5. Personalization and AI-driven Recommendations
- Tailored User Experience: How Pinterest might utilize AI and machine learning to offer hyper-personalized content feeds to users.
- Brands and Personalization: Leveraging AI-driven insights to tailor your brand content to specific audience segments.

6. Augmented Reality (AR) and Virtual Reality (VR) on Pinterest
- AR Shopping Experiences: Envisioning a future where users can virtually "try on" products using AR.
- VR Inspirational Boards: The potential for immersive virtual boards where users can step into their dream spaces.

7. Sustainability and Social Responsibility Trends
- Eco-conscious Boards: The rise of boards dedicated to sustainable living, eco-friendly products, and social responsibility.
- Brands and Social Responsibility: How brands can align with these values and cater to an audience increasingly conscious of sustainability

8. Expanding Global Reach
- Localization and Regional Content: Pinterest's potential expansions into new geographical markets and the implications for brands.
- Multilingual Content: The importance of catering to a diverse, global audience with multilingual pins and boards.

9. Enhanced Analytics and Data Insights
- Deeper Audience Insights: Predicting advancements in Pinterest Analytics that offer richer insights into user behavior and preferences.
- Brands and Data-Driven Decisions: Utilizing these insights for more informed content and marketing strategies.

10. Evolving Advertising Opportunities
- Dynamic Ads: The potential of AI-driven ads that adapt in real-time based on user behavior and preferences.

- VR and AR Advertising: Considering the future of immersive advertising experiences on Pinterest, allowing users to virtually interact with products before purchase.

11. Voice Search and Integration

- The Role of Voice Assistants: Anticipating the integration of voice search within Pinterest and its impact on search behavior.
- Optimizing for Voice: Strategies for brands to ensure their content remains discoverable as voice-driven searches increase.

12. Community Building and Engagement

- Enhanced Group Boards: Predicting advancements in group board features that foster more substantial community interactions and collaborations.
- Direct Engagements: Future tools that might allow brands to engage directly with their followers, facilitating deeper connections and feedback loops.

13. Sustainability of Organic Reach

- Shifts in Algorithm: Recognizing the potential of algorithms to increasingly favor paid content, mirroring trends observed on other platforms.
- Strategies for Organic Visibility: Tips and tactics to ensure your brand's content remains visible in an ever-competitive environment.

14. Security and Privacy Concerns

- Data Privacy: As the digital world becomes increasingly data-driven, understanding potential changes in Pinterest's data privacy policies and user controls.
- Brand Responsibility: Ensuring brands handle user data with integrity and transparency, respecting evolving norms and regulations.

15. Integration with Other Social Platforms

- Cross-Platform Campaigns: The potential for deeper integrations with platforms like Instagram, Facebook, or TikTok, allowing for more cohesive cross-platform marketing campaigns.
- Unified Analytics: Envisioning a future where analytics tools provide insights that span multiple platforms, offering a holistic view of brand reach and engagement.

Concluding Thoughts for Chapter 18

As we look to the future of Pinterest marketing, it's clear that the platform will continue to evolve, bringing both new opportunities and challenges for brands. Success will hinge on a brand's ability to adapt, innovate, and stay attuned to the platform's shifts and its audience's changing needs. In this ever-changing landscape, a blend of foresight, flexibility, and a commitment to genuine engagement will guide brands to continued growth and success on Pinterest.

In the upcoming chapter, we will delve into case studies, showcasing real-world examples of brands that have masterfully leveraged Pinterest for marketing success. These stories will offer valuable insights, lessons learned, and inspiration for your brand's Pinterest journey.

Chapter 19: Case Studies - Brands that Mastered Pinterest

To truly grasp the potential of Pinterest and understand how the platform can be harnessed effectively, it's invaluable to examine real-world success stories. In this chapter, we'll delve into a selection of brands that have strategically leveraged Pinterest to boost their brand presence, drive engagement, and achieve their marketing goals.

1. Introduction: Learning from the Best
   • Real-World Insights: The importance of studying actual brand campaigns to gather practical insights and strategies.
   • Diverse Approaches: Recognizing that there's no one-size-fits-all strategy, and success on Pinterest can come in various forms.
2. Glossier: Crafting a Visual Brand Story
   • Visual Consistency: How Glossier maintained a cohesive visual aesthetic that mirrored their brand identity across all pins and boards.

- Engaging Tutorials: The use of video pins to demonstrate product applications, driving both engagement and sales.

3. Wayfair: Leveraging Shop the Look Pins
- Home Decor Inspirations: How Wayfair created engaging mood boards for different home decor themes, linking products directly with Shop the Look pins.
- User-Generated Content: Encouraging users to share their own home setups featuring Wayfair products, creating an authentic brand community.

4. Airbnb: Promoting Destination Boards
- Travel Dreaming: Curating boards based on popular travel destinations, providing users with travel inspirations linked to Airbnb listings.
- Storytelling: Utilizing user reviews and stories to create engaging travel narratives for each destination.

5. Ben & Jerry's: Tapping into Seasonal Trends
- Seasonal Boards: Creating themed boards around seasons or holidays, such as "Summer Chill with Ben & Jerry's" or "Halloween Treats."
- Interactive Contests: Encouraging users to submit their own ice cream flavor ideas or dessert recipes.

6. Lowe's: DIY Projects and Tutorials
- Practical Guidance: Offering step-by-step guides and tutorials for home improvement projects, positioning Lowe's as a go-to resource.
- Video Demonstrations: Using video pins to visually guide users through various DIY projects, driving both engagement and in-store sales.

7. Whole Foods: Recipe Inspirations and Health Tips
- Healthy Eating Boards: Curating boards with recipes using ingredients available at Whole Foods, encouraging users to try them out.
- Sustainability Focus: Promoting eco-friendly products and sharing tips on sustainable living.

8. Nike Women: Empowering Through Inspiration
- Fitness Goals and Aspirations: Curating boards that feature workout plans, motivational quotes, and product recommendations tailored for women.

- Behind-the-Scenes: Sharing exclusive behind-the-scenes content from product shoots and events to engage and build a closer connection with their audience.

9. Sephora: Beauty Tutorials and Product Showcases
- Diverse Beauty Standards: Emphasizing inclusivity by featuring models of various ethnicities, sizes, and styles.
- Interactive Beauty Quizzes: Directing users to quizzes that recommend products based on skin type, preferences, and concerns, seamlessly integrating e-commerce.

10. REI: Adventure and Outdoor Living
- Adventure Boards: Crafting boards around different outdoor activities like hiking, camping, and kayaking, guiding users on essential gear and tips.
- Sustainability Initiatives: Showcasing their eco-friendly products and commitment to sustainable business practices, resonating with conscious consumers.

11. LEGO: Beyond Just Building Blocks
- Creative Inspirations: Offering unique building ideas and challenges to foster creativity among users of all ages.
- Engaging with Fan Creations: Encouraging the LEGO community to share their creations, then spotlighting these fan-made designs on their official boards.

12. Tasty by BuzzFeed: Viral Recipe Videos
- Bite-sized Video Content: Sharing short, visually appealing recipe videos that users can easily replicate at home.
- Interactive Polls and Challenges: Hosting periodic polls, asking users to vote on their next recipe or challenge them to recreate dishes.

13. Madewell: Fashion Trends and Styling Tips
- Lookbook Inspirations: Regularly updating their boards with the latest fashion trends, helping users curate their style.
- User Testimonials: Featuring real users showcasing Madewell products, adding an authentic touch to their brand image.

14. The New York Times: Diversifying Content Strategy

- Thematic Boards: Curating articles around themes such as "Travel", "Food", or "Books", catering to varied interests.
- Infographics and Visual Stories: Leveraging Pinterest's visual format to share striking infographics and condensed news stories, driving traffic back to their main site.

Concluding Thoughts for Chapter 18

These case studies not only highlight the adaptability of Pinterest as a platform for various industries but also emphasize the importance of genuine, value-driven content. Brands that see beyond direct selling and prioritize engagement, education, or inspiration tend to resonate most with Pinterest users.

Remember, the Pinterest audience seeks meaningful connections and authentic interactions. By understanding and empathizing with their needs, brands can craft a strategy that not only drives traffic and sales but also fosters loyalty and brand advocacy.

Chapter 20: Concluding Reflections - Setting the Path Forward in Pinterest Marketing

As we reach the concluding chapter of "Pin to Profit: Mastering the Art of Monetizing Pinterest," it's vital to synthesize the insights, strategies, and principles we've explored. This chapter is designed to offer a consolidated perspective, anchoring your understanding and setting you on a clear path forward.

1. Introduction: The Essence of Pinterest Marketing
- A Unique Platform: Recognizing that Pinterest, at its core, is about inspiration, discovery, and aspiration. Its users come with an intent – to be inspired, to discover something new, and to manifest those aspirations into reality.

2. The Fundamentals Revisited
- Purposeful Pinning: The importance of creating pins that not only capture attention but also provide value and purpose to the audience.

- Audience Understanding: Grasping the significance of in-depth audience research and crafting content that truly resonates with them.
- Adapting to Evolutions: Being open to the platform's changes and ensuring that your strategies evolve alongside Pinterest's features and algorithms.

3. The Power of Authenticity
- Beyond Sales: Recognizing that genuine connections and brand trust often drive long-term success more than direct sales.
- Storytelling: The undeniable impact of creating a strong, authentic narrative around your brand or products.

4. Lessons from the Field
- Case Study Insights: Reiterating the importance of learning from real-world successes and failures, gleaning actionable insights from other brands' experiences.
- Pivoting and Adapting: Being open to change and having the agility to adjust strategies based on performance data and feedback.

5. Preparing for the Future
- Embracing Innovations: As Pinterest introduces new features or tools, the necessity of staying updated and leveraging them to your advantage.
- Continued Learning: The digital marketing landscape is ever-evolving. Dedicate time to continuous learning, be it through courses, webinars, or peer discussions.

6. The Importance of Community
- Building Relationships: The true power of Pinterest lies in community engagement. Prioritize building relationships over mere follower counts.
- Feedback Loops: Regularly solicit feedback and engage in two-way conversations with your audience, ensuring your strategies remain aligned with their needs.

7. Final Thoughts and Parting Advice
- Consistency is Key: Regular pinning, consistent branding, and sustained audience engagement can pave the way for long-term success.

- Stay Inspired: Just as users come to Pinterest for inspiration, brands too should seek inspiration. Be open to exploring new creative avenues, styles, or content formats.
- Commitment to Value: Always prioritize providing genuine value to your audience, whether it's through informative content, problem-solving products, or engaging interactions.

8. Practical Tips for Sustained Success

- Regular Audits: Make it a practice to periodically review your Pinterest account, analyzing which pins or boards are performing best, and understanding why. This helps refine your strategy and ensures you're consistently delivering high-quality content.
- Diversify Content: While it's crucial to maintain brand consistency, it's equally important to experiment with different types of content – infographics, videos, user-generated content, and more. This keeps your profile fresh and caters to a wider audience.
- Collaborate and Co-create: Consider partnering with other brands or influencers in your niche for pin collaborations or joint boards. This not only brings fresh perspectives but also exposes your brand to a wider audience.

9. Overcoming Challenges and Setbacks

- Stay Resilient: Like any marketing platform, Pinterest will have its highs and lows. Remember that occasional setbacks are a part of the journey. What's crucial is learning from them and adapting.
- Seek Community Support: Engage with other brands or marketers on Pinterest, join forums or communities, and don't hesitate to ask questions or share experiences. The collective wisdom can be a powerful tool in navigating challenges.

10. Beyond Pinterest: Integrating with Other Platforms

- Holistic Digital Strategy: While this guide focuses on Pinterest, remember that it's just one piece of the puzzle. Consider how Pinterest fits into your broader digital marketing strategy, and ensure there's synergy across platforms.

- Cross-Promotion: Use other platforms, be it Instagram, Facebook, or your brand's blog, to promote your Pinterest profile and vice versa. A cohesive multi-platform presence amplifies your brand's reach and engagement.

11. Commitment to Continued Growth

- Stay Curious: The digital landscape is continuously evolving. Make it a habit to stay updated with the latest trends, tools, and best practices.
- Invest in Learning: Consider dedicated Pinterest training sessions, webinars, or workshops. As the platform grows, there will always be new techniques and strategies to explore.

A Journey, Not a Destination

Mastering Pinterest marketing is an ongoing process. As you continue to engage with the platform, you'll discover new insights, face novel challenges, and uncover fresh opportunities. It's a dynamic journey, one that requires patience, persistence, and passion.

Remember, at its core, Pinterest is a platform of dreams, desires, and discoveries. As a brand, your role is to inspire, guide, and be a part of those dreams. Approach Pinterest with an open heart, a creative mind, and a commitment to genuine value.

As we wrap up this guide, we leave you with a quote that encapsulates the spirit of Pinterest: "The future belongs to those who believe in the beauty of their dreams." - Eleanor Roosevelt.

Here's to your dreams, your aspirations, and your continued success on Pinterest and beyond.

Conclusion: Embarking on Your Pinterest Odyssey

In the expansive universe of Pinterest, we've embarked on a profound journey, delving deep into the heartbeats of inspiration and the whispers of aspirations. This isn't merely a platform of pins, but a canvas for dreams, hopes, and the powerful stories waiting to be told. With every strategy we've uncovered and every tale we've shared, the essence remains clear: your authenticity, creativity, and passion are the pillars of your Pinterest success.

Navigating this dynamic landscape requires more than just tools and tactics. It demands a visionary spirit, a heart willing to listen, and the courage to adapt and evolve. Every pin you craft, every board you curate, is a testament to your brand's legacy and the impact you wish to make.

Remember, in the ever-shifting dance of the digital realm, the most resonant notes are those sung with genuine emotion and intention. As this guide concludes, understand that your Pinterest journey is just beginning. There's an entire world of inspiration awaiting your touch.

Let Pinterest be the gallery where your brand's artistry shines, where your narratives captivate, and where dreams find their wings. Step forth with confidence, embrace the journey, and etch your indelible mark. Here's to a future painted with your visions and a legacy sculpted one pin at a time. Shine brilliantly, and let the world revel in your Pinterest magic.

www.ingramcontent.com/pod-product-compliance
Lightning Source LLC
Chambersburg PA
CBHW062242290526
45794CB00006B/2366